"This book is a powerful instrument to stay focused on whatever you want to accomplish in life. Whether you use it for improving your personal life or your career, it defines goals in a way and then helps you formulate specific actions on how to achieve them. There are a variety of examples of other people's experiences in using these tools to which I was able to relate. I was inspired to pattern my own personal worksheet. The book is such a complete guide that it seems Stacey is actually coming out from the pages coaching and supporting you. A must-have book for everybody for shaping one's life destiny and purpose."

Cynthia De Los Reyes, RN, LMT,
Raindrop Technique Practitioner

"Chi-To-be is a great accomplishment. Stacey Hall has created a fun, easy-to-follow road map on the most difficult passage of life...the road to personal fulfillment. Using her navigation tools you will find your way of avoiding the pitfalls of stress, uncertainty and misalignment. This is of the highest value. For what good is arriving to your destination, frazzled, unhealthy and alone? Cheers, Stacey, and thank you for sharing your journey and the lessons you have learned for the rest of us to follow. See you on the Beach!!!"

Jeff Stewart, CEO, The Nia Technique Inc.
Changing People's Lives Through Movement Since 1983

"If you know there is more you want to do in this life and you want to stop struggling with determining what you are called to do/be, this amazing book will help you to easily discover the answer. Stacey helps seekers find their path and offers proven techniques for success. Enjoy the ride!"

Carol Mittwede, Owner, Northwest Yoga Studio
www.northwestyogastudio.com
NIA student

"Chi-To-Be! is uplifting and easy to read. I love how it starts at 'the end' by helping me to focus on my final goal and providing ways to keep me moving forward without getting discouraged. This book helped me and it will help you, too!"

Kaye Lynne Murphy, LMT
Raindrop Technique Practitioner
www.kayelynne.com

"*Stacey Hall, author, life coach, teacher, friend – is one of those rare people that practices what she preaches. She is a fearless warrior when it comes to following and achieving her life's goal and hearts' desire. Her example and the principles in her book are life-changing, thought-provoking and supported me in examining my approach to achieving my personal and professional goals and intentions by helping me sort through and choose the commitments that will serve me best. She has helped me unlock and discover my potential. I went from being a very content NIA student to becoming the first NIA Instructor in my city to now having a B-All of sprouting more NIA teachers. I intend to travel through Europe, teaching NIA wherever I can. Because of Stacey, I am a happy, brave, proud, blessed, fearless woman, teacher and warrior. I have achieved extraordinary results and personal fulfillment. Thank you Stacey, because of you, I not only dream big, I believe BIG!*"

Kathy McKean, NIA Instructor

"*Stacey Hall's book, CHI-TO-BE! is a MUST HAVE tool that opens the unchartered waters of incredible success in anything we choose to create. Want the real secrets of achieving fulfillment spiritually, emotionally, financially and more? This is a must read. Of all "the how to" succeed books, this is by far, the clearest, simplest to follow and actually do! A perfect gift for everyone I know. A gift from Stacey Hall's soul to ours.*"

Nancy Orlen Weber, RN, CCA, CRTI,
Medical Intuitive, Certified Clinical
Aromatherapist, Animal Communicator,
Psychic Detective (documentaries on TV worldwide)
www.nancyorlenweber.com

"Such an insightful, well-articulated, and practical read! Grabbed me right from the beginning and didn't let go. Stacey has a way of taking the intangible and turning it into the absolutely attainable. Do yourself a favor and schedule your success!"

Jamison Duhon, Hair Stylist

"As a hands-on healer for over half of my life, I have grown to know how imperative it is to keep a harmonized balance within myself in order to give a high quality of healing and life force energy to others. I feel that everything is possible for us all when we maintain integrity and balance in ourselves. If we pay attention to our lives, we can clearly see if we are in harmony and balance by our success and results.

To do this, I ask myself, 'Do I feel empowered today?' Staying in and maintaining balance requires necessary daily action...whether it's meditating, sleeping more, exercising, taking time to regenerate in nature, expanding our own consciousness etc... Balance is everything to me. It has become one of my greatest values within myself.

I also feel it truly helps to have someone in our lives that is a living example of true empowerment. For me, this is Stacey Hall. She lives her life in such profound integrity and has garnered incredible wisdom that literally inspires, uplifts and changes lives on so many levels. I believe she is a wise woman who truly walks her talk!"

Julie Chertow,
Bodyworker/Healer/Educator
Ashland, Oregon
www.BodyAliveEssentials.com

CHI-TO-BEI

CHI-TO-BE!

ACHIEVING YOUR ULTIMATE *B-ALL*

STACEY HALL

Generating Abundant Energy
to Achieve Your Goals
With Velocity and Ease

LIFE SCIENCE PUBLISHING™

Life Science Publishing ISBN 978-0-615-46801-3

10 9 8 7 6 5 4 3 2

For more information about custom editions, special sales, premium and corporate purchases, please contact Life Science Publishing at (800) 336-6308 or www.lifesciencepublishers.com

LIFE SCIENCE PUBLISHING™
YESTERDAY'S WISDOM· TODAY'S DISCOVERY

Table of Contents

Dedication

I dedicate this book to the Divine Power within us all!

● ● ● ● ● ● ●
[
*"Whatever you can do, or
dream you can, begin it.
Boldness has genius, power,
and magic in it."*
– *Johann Wolfgang von Goethe*
]

Acknowledgements

As this book and its accompanying **Chi-To-Be! Mastery™**
coaching program have been developed over my entire life thus
far, the acknowledgements of appreciation I have to express
would fill another entire book if I were to list everyone
individually.

First and foremost, I acknowledge and appreciate the support
and constant guidance I receive from God, the Divine Creator,
the Gracious, the Powerful, the Generous, the Loving! Also, I
acknowledge and appreciate the wisdom and guidance received
from the Angelic Realm and the Great Prophets and Masters
who inspire me daily.

Next, to everyone I have ever attracted into my life – my family,
friends, clients, coaches, teachers, healers, business and
brainstorming partners, my Young Living® team members,
everyone – Thank you! I appreciate each and every one of you
and your contributions to my life and well-being.

For the development of this book and the **Chi-To-Be! Mastery
Program** specifically, I acknowledge and appreciate my own
contributions and those of my husband, Bill Hall, as well as each
of the following great souls listed in alphabetical order whose
support, endorsement, and other ways of generating abundant
energy have been equally important.

Carlos AyaRosas, The Nia Technique

Chef Mayra

Troie Battles, Life Science Publishing, LLC

Olivia Biera, OPB Consulting, Chi-To-Be! Master

Lloydine Burris

Nichola Burnett, R.D.

Karen Marie Campbell, The Spirit Within U

Kelly Case, Young Living®

Julie Chertow, Bodyworker/Healer/Educator

Brandon Christensen, Director/Editor

Terah Kathryn Collins, best-selling author and
    founder of the Western School of Feng Shui

Cynthia De Los Rosas, RN, LMT

Jamison Duhon, Hair Stylist

Jackie Evon, Fleming's Prime Steakhouse & Wine Bar

Diana Ewald, Ordained Minister

Skip Fox, Fleming's Prime Steakhouse & Wine Bar

John Gilbert, Ph.D.

Amber J. Griffiths, AGDesign

Jonathan Barrick Griffiths, Composer/Manager

Tracy Griffiths, RPP, RPE, CMT

Maggie Hall

Sunny Hall

Tess Hall

Loralee Humpherys, LMT, Chi-To-Be! Master

Maria Jackson, LMT, BA, MA, Chi-To-Be! Master

Jason Jensen, Life Science Publishing, LLC

Lauren Kling, Chi-To-Be! Master

Christina Lindley, Chi-To-Be! Master

Vicki Luckman

Melinda Macleod, Bio-Feedback Specialist,
    Certified Business/Life Coach

Warren R. Markowitz, Esq.

Kathy McKean, NIA Instructor

Carolyn Mein, D.C.

Denise Michaels, Author, 'Marketing Maven'

Kaye Lynne Murphy, LMT, Raindrop Technique
    Practitioner

Joey Melotti, Dreamspell Studios

Valerie Melotti, Dreamspell Studios, Chi-To-Be! Master

Carol Mittwede, Northwest Yoga Studio

Tim Moreno, P.E.

Dez O'Connor, Reiki Master, "The Rose Quartz Healing
    Mentor," Chi-To-Be! Master

Nancy Orlen Weber, RN, CCA, CRTI

Jackie Olsen, LSHC, CAC

Stacey Pangburn-Jaynes, Photographer

Amelia Pawlak, Founder of 'Your Perfect Role'

Steve Piersanti, Berrett-Koehler Publishers, Inc.

Patricia Pincus

Linda Kavelin Popov, The Virtues Project International

Mike Rayburn, World's Funniest Guitar Virtuoso

Tara Rayburn, "The Healthy Habit Coach",
Chi-To-Be! Master

Mark Richardson, Kolrich Associates, for the most
perfect cover design

Debbie Rosas, The Nia Technique

Tina Rose

Jacob Rhythmic Dragon, Foundation for the
Law of Time

Nicolette Salamanca, Hay House, Inc.

Barbara Sanchez

Sandra Lee Schubert, MSC, Chi-To-Be! Master

Jennifer Shulte, LMT, NCTMB

Laura Siderman, Gypsywing.com

Jeevan Sivasubramaniam, Berrett-Koehler Publishers, Inc

Arturo Soza, Life Science Publishing, LLC.

Corey Stallings, Chi-To-Be! Master

Boyd Michael Staszewski

David Stewart, Ph.D., D.N.M

Jeff Stewart, CEO, The Nia Technique Inc.

Michael Thrower, LSH/CRP/CAC, Chi-To-Be! Master

Marcella Vonn Harting, PH.Dc

Donna Wheatcroft, B.Ed.

Janet Womack

D. Gary Young, Young Living®

Mary Young, Young Living®

Foreword
by Marcella Vonn Harting

It is with great pleasure that I accepted to write the foreword for Stacey for a book that demands our personal involvement in understanding the WHY to our success and the importance of maintaining balance to sustain our successes. I believe the quality of your life may well be a function of the why you do what you do. The only difference between where you are now and where you choose to be is why you do what you do! This book is full of thoughts and questions that will lead you into an inward search for meaning and application to get your WHY. Stacey's provocative voice of wisdom and strategies places you right on the journey to success. This book is a thought-provoking blueprint and support system to success. The secret is the system, which for me stands for 'save yourself, time, energy and money'.

As a top leader in an International MLM company, I am asked all the time, "What do I do to get where you are?" I can tell them in great detail how to get to where I am, but if their WHY isn't as compelling as mine, they usually do not succeed. Stacey gives you a step-by-step approach in a collection of exercises and experiences designed to explore and fully awaken your mind, body and spirit to your heart's desires. Perhaps this book's greatest value is that it assists you in creating your plan to manage success on a physical, emotional and spiritual level. Her **'Chi-To-Be!™**, Generating Abundant Energy to Achieve Your *B-All'* approach evolves every aspect of our lives so that we can sustain and maintain our success and easily manage more abundance.

The importance of maintaining balance to sustain our success encourages us to move beyond misperceived limitations and re-write new empowering identities for ourselves....breaking through our mental and emotional restrictions we place upon ourselves, and attracting more abundance with Grace and Ease.

This book's time is NOW, for you to find your voice, to become the solution and to make a difference. We all have the ability to make memories and change lives. By applying these principles to your personal life, you can lead a life that is purposeful, self-directed and aligned with who you truly are!

Take a look at your own life and ask yourself, are you where you choose to be? Are you healthy, financially secure or happy in your relationships? Keep asking and you will understand you are where you are today because of the decisions and priorities you choose to focus on.

Through my own life experiences I have learned that the past does not make the future. If you are not where you choose to be, then do something about it.

Success leaves clues. You have in your hands the blueprint for a successful journey. Be the leader of your own life and take action with the strategies and tools in this book.

Energized, Empowered and Transformed,

Marcella Vonn Harting, PH.Dc
Ph.D. Candidate in Psychoneurology & Integrative Medicine
Crown Diamond, Young Living® Essential Oils
480-443-3224

www.MARCELLAVONNHARTING.com
mvonn@aol.com

Introduction

$$\bullet\ \bullet\ \bullet\ \bullet\ \bullet\ \bullet\ \bullet\ \bullet\ \bullet \quad \left[\begin{array}{c} \text{"}I \text{ want to learn how to heal my heart} \\ \text{and then help others to heal theirs!"} \end{array} \right]$$

This was the desperate plea that burst forth from my lips one day when I had reached a point of complete physical, emotional and mental depletion following eight years of experiencing the highest highs and lowest lows of my life.

Those words launched me on a six-year journey of self-discovery that I now know will be life-long.

This book is an opportunity to take a **rest stop** (see Chapter 9) for me on this journey so I may share with you what I have learned so far.

In 1996, I began sharing with my clients a process I created for tapping into the Law of Attraction. I share more about this process in Chapter 4. By 2001, this process had been shared with thousands of people and was introduced world-wide in *'Attracting Perfect Customers...The Power of Strategic Synchronicity'*. Over the next few years, I experienced the joy of fulfillment at having co-authored a best-selling book and the co-creation of a coaching and consulting company based on this transformational process I created.

Yet, in the fall of 2004, I physically, emotionally, and mentally had run out of energy and enthusiasm to take these accomplishments to the next level of success.

As I began to acknowledge and address my lack of energy, I experienced a huge blow to my emotions. My father passed away suddenly on October 7, 2004. Although he had suffered a stroke 5 years previously, over his last six months he had shown signs of improvement in his recovery. So, there was nothing to indicate that the day he died would be his last one on earth. My father was one of my strongest supporters and I felt as if I had a huge hole in my heart and my life after his passing. I also had tremendous guilt because a week before he died, he had asked me to come visit soon and I told him *"I had too much to do for the business"* to fly out right then. Since I already had plans to visit my family in December, I actually said to him, *"We'll be together for the holidays. It's not like you're dying."*

Little did I know!

The burden of guilt that I added to my already-depleted body was the literal straw that broke the camel's back. I had tremendous difficulty getting out of bed each morning. Physically, my body felt like it had been hit with a 2' by 4'. Emotionally, I felt powerless. Mentally, I had run out of ideas and my creativity was non-existent.

Never before had I ever been in such a state. I was always the go-getter, the over-achiever, the busy person who could always get things done no matter how much was on her plate. I had no idea what was happening to me. All I knew was that I could no longer provide coaching or support to others while I was in such a depleted state myself.

I chose to relinquish my shares in the company I had birthed – another heart-wrenching decision – and make myself my own #1 client for the first time in my life.

There were months when I did not get out of bed. I sought support from coaches, nutritionists, and doctors of alternative medicine. My blood pressure was sky-high and my liver was full of toxins. I changed my diet completely – choosing to eat gluten-free – and I noticed that as I changed my eating habits, my body and my mind began to feel stronger and I was able to deal with the emotions that had previously been too painful to feel.

I read self-help books, I attended life-affirming workshops and seminars, and I made it a point to watch 'The Ellen Show' every day at 3:00 p.m. because I could always count on laughing at least once during every show. And, laughing made my heart feel better.

And, little by little, I began to feel happier.

However, by this time, I was doing nothing physically active. So I found a NIA™ class close to home and began taking, and then teaching, Nia Technique™ classes to strengthen my body, mind, emotions and spirit. At one of the locations where I taught, I was invited to attend a class on using Young Living® essential oils (www.youngliving.org/chitobe). The minute I opened the door to the classroom and the delicious aromas greeted my nose, I knew that I was in the right place. It was as if every pore on my body had a little mouth and they were all drinking in as much of the scent as possible. Intuitively, I knew that these oils would be an important tool in healing my heart…and helping others heal theirs, too.

And, that is exactly what has happened.

What I have learned through this journey is the importance of maintaining my physical, emotional, and mental energy at a consistently high vibration in order to achieve all of my **goals**. In other words, I have learned how to keep my 'Chi' ("life-force") flowing around and through all of my bodies so they now function as one unit.

I learned that clinical research has proven that essential oils have the highest frequency of any natural substance known to man and that by applying essential oils to my body, I am increasing cellular frequency and circulation, which increases oxygen delivery to the cell. Basically, each time I am inhaling pure essential oils or applying them to my body, I am literally giving myself more power and strength...or as I like to say, and the title of this book, conveys...I am increasing my Chi energy to be and do whatever I desire!

I was also inspired when I learned that Bruce Tainio of Tainio Technology in Cheney, Washington, developed new equipment to measure the biofrequency of humans and foods. He used this biofrequency monitor to measured the influence that thoughts have on the body's electrical frequency.

I was amazed to learn that negative thoughts lowered the measured frequency by 12 MHz and positive thoughts raised the measured frequency by 10 MHz. It was also found that prayer and meditation increased the measured frequency levels by 15 MHz.

So, I began to focus my attention on how to maintain my body's biofrequency at its highest level through positive thinking and various other methods to increase my Chi energy. As a result, my health continued to increase, my energy returned to full strength, and my mind began to function clearly again.

$$\left[\begin{array}{c} \textit{"I have been able to heal} \\ \textit{my heart - both physically} \\ \textit{and emotionally..."} \end{array}\right]$$

• • • • • • • • •

I consider the **11 Chi-To-Be! Energy Surges** I share in this book as the essential tools, resources, support and nutrients with which I nourished and nurtured my body, mind, emotions and spirit to bring me to a level of well-being I did not know existed – or was not even possible for me to experience – six years ago.

I am now a Certified Aromatherapy Coach and a Licensed Spiritual Healer on my way to attaining a doctorate in Natural Medicine (my *B-All*, to be explained in Chapter 1).

And, as I declared six years ago, I have been able to heal my heart – both physically and emotionally – as well as being blessed to be able to share these tools with many great souls to support them in healing their hearts and achieving their own life's **goals**.

You will meet a few of these masterful leaders throughout this book. Each one is a participant in the **Chi-To-Be! Masters™** coaching program, which you will learn more about in Chapter 13.

As you enter in the process of generating your own Chi energy to achieve your ultimate *B-All*, I invite you to first turn to Chapter 12 where you will find a **Chi Generator Calculator.** Use this Calculator as your guide for amping-up, balancing and grounding your energy as you utilize the tools available in each chapter of this book.

Blessings of powerful joy to you!

Stacey Hall
February 2011

Attracting Perfect Customers, The Power of Strategic Synchronicity by Stacey Hall and Jan Brogniez, copyright © by Stacey Hall and Jan Brogniez, Published by Berrett-Koehler Publishers, Inc.

The Yin and Yang of Chi-To-Be!

As you begin to read the first chapter of this book, you will experience a sense of being taken on a personal journey of discovery.

On each and every page, you will discover tips (which I call 'Energy Surges') for generating the power and maintaining the momentum required for achieving each and every one of your goals and desires.

And, you will also discover that there is no mysterious 'secret' to attaining success.

Every road to success is paved with systematic patterns and procedures. I share these simple systems with you in Chapters 1 - 4. These chapters comprise the *yang* half of the book as you will be engaged in *self-analytical, interactive* exercises designed to support you in discovering – very specifically – what it is you are committed to achieving in this lifetime.

The terms you will discover in these first 4 chapters will be used and highlighted throughout the book.

Look for these terms and use them as your guideposts for remaining on the shortest path to the achievement of your goals as you experience the adventures provided by the *yin* **Chi-To-Be! Energy Surges** in Chapters 5 - 13. Each one is an invitation to increase your inner power and give yourself an energy burst to reach your next highest level of success with velocity and ease.

Utilizing these yin and yang energies – form and flow, masculine and feminine, action and rest – in harmony will bring balance to all aspects of your life making your journey enjoyable and personally satisfying….in addition to being successful.

Be Empowered – Be Powerful – Keep Your Eye on Your *B-All!*

chapter 1
Starting at the End of it All

I've always believed that the best place to start is at the end!
Or, as I like to paraphrase the old saying –

● ● ● ● ● ● ● ● ●
$$\left[\begin{array}{c} \textit{"if you don't know where you are going,} \\ \textit{you are sure to end up} \\ \textit{where you don't want to be."} \end{array}\right]$$

This is why I want to be sure I know where I want to end up
before I start any project! By knowing where I want to end up, I
am able to map out the course I plan to take to get there as
quickly as possible.

And, I can also plan in advance what tools, resources, support
and nutrients I will require to keep my energy full and vibrant
throughout the process.

So, let's now begin at the end together.

STARTING AT THE END

My first invitation of the many you will receive throughout this
book is to take a moment to consider what you feel you must
accomplish before the end of your life here on earth. Yes,
before you leave the earth.

Remember, I said we would be starting at the end!

Once you have your answer, we can lighten up and have some fun.

Next, please take out a sheet of paper and make a list of all the projects, activities, and commitments you have made to yourself to achieve before your body is ready to move on to whatever is next.

The next step is to put a circle around the top 3 projects, activities and/or commitments that you have listed – the ones you feel are **ABSOLUTE MUSTS** for you to accomplish in this lifetime.

Your 3rd step is to consider – of those 3 that are circled – which is the **ABSOLUTE #1** – this is the one I like to call my "*B-All*" (said as **'Be-All'** - a shortened version of the phrase 'be-all, end-all') **Goal**.

Your "*B-All*" **Goal** – henceforth known as your '*B-All*" – is what you will be keeping your eye on throughout this book until it's achieved.

This is the end at which we will begin!

So to reach your Ultimate **Goal** – throughout this book – "Keep Your Eye on Your *B-All*"!

KEEP ONE'S EYE ON THE BALL
1. Fig. to watch or follow the ball carefully, especially when one is playing a ball game; to follow the details of a ball game very carefully.
2. Fig. to remain alert to the events occurring around oneself.

McGraw-Hill Dictionary of American Idioms and Phrasal Verbs.
© 2002 by The McGraw-Hill Companies, Inc

GOALS AND INTENTIONS TO FULFILL THE *B-All*

I have found over the course of the many years that I have been fortunate to coach others in achieving their *B-All* that most people are confused as to the difference between a **goal** and an **intention**.

And, depending upon the number of people who you ask – you will get as many different explanations and definitions of these two terms.

For the purposes of this book, I ask for you to accept that I have a distinct difference when I say '**goal**' versus 'intention'.

For me, a **goal** is like the finish line. When I say I have a **goal**, it's the place I want to end up. If I was playing baseball, it would be home plate. If it was football, it would be the end zone.

> *It's the specific place –*
> *the actual destination – that*
> *is my definition of a* goal.

Why? This is because the achievement of the **goal** brings you one step closer to the fulfillment of your *B-All*. You will have many important **goals** to achieve before you ultimately fulfill your *B-All*.

CONTRIBUTIONS FROM THE CHI-TO-BE! MASTERS

To assist you in identifying your own *B-All*, here are the *B-Alls* and one Top **Goal** for each of the **Chi-To-Be! Masters:**

 Christina L.

B-All: To win a major televised live poker tournament for over 1 Million Dollars.

Goal: I intend to get on a regular workout routine so that my body is as prepared as my mind, working out for a minimum of 4 times a week for 45 minutes.

 Olivia B.

B-All: To ensure my daughter's well being, prosperity, health and strong spiritual connection, while refining my own through core connection to Highest Truth and Deepest Body Consciousness so that we are able to do the work necessary to hold the Earth in balance.

Goal: To pay off my mortgage.

 DeZ O.

B-All: To be financially independent in order to be of service to others to support them to recognize the Divine Power within them for empowering themselves to live joyously in the adventure of reaching their own *B-All* in-joy and appreciation.

Goal: Becoming abundantly successful by empowering mind, body and soul wellbeing in others as a Young Living® Entrepreneur!

Valerie M.

B-All: To support people so they can make educated choices about their health and their treatments.

Goal: Completely move into and organize my office.

 Lauren K.

B-All: To change the world and people's lives in a positive and influential way and thus be financially successful and extremely happy.

Goal: Work out a mutually-beneficial deal with my sponsor where I have a separate live and online backing deal and he backs me to play in major live tournaments.

 Loralee H.

B-All: To create an online Educational and Wellness Center that Teaches, Touches and Trains individuals, inspiring a change of consciousness in them that leads to lifestyle behaviors and habits that encourage and support Health and Longevity.

Goal: Hold a successful monthly class with 8+ people in attendance.

 Maria J.

B-All: Building a refuge for those who have found Western medicine has failed them.

Goal: To finish construction on my first url: http://www.healthyanti-agingwarrior.com.

Michael T.

B-All: To reach the ultimate state of enlightenment for me and others.

Goal: To build financial freedom in the development of my Young Living® business.

Sandra S.

B-All: I am known for my great work that inspires and motivates people to create their own great work and live an inspired life.

Goal: Book two clients into my 'The Business Monthly Maintenance' package.

Corey S.

B-All: To create my successful entertainment company. The company will bring a high level of artistry back into the entertainment industry and attract artists who are unwilling to compromise their art for money.

Goal: Start recording my own music and begin to attract like minds.

Tara R.

B-All: I have and continue to circulate $1 million dollars in the bank to use for helping others in the ways I am guided by God.

Goal: To develop a 'Healthy Living Coaching' online classroom course.

The extent to which a **goal** can be fulfilled is dependent upon the amount of **intention** that is committed towards the achievement of that **goal**.

An "**intention**" – in my world – is the motivation and the commitment to achieve the **goal**. Intention is the power (Chi energy) directed into the fulfillment of the **goal**.

Intentions are the 'why' we schedule all the planned activities, conversations, meetings, and projects we create to achieve each one of the **goals** on our way to achieving our *B-All*.

And, all those planned conversations, activities, meetings and projects will now be known as **intentional activities** and each will have a 'by when' date attached to it! A 'by when' date is the date by which you want to complete each **intentional activity** so that the **goal** can be achieved as quickly as possible – so that your ultimate *B-All* is fulfilled with velocity and ease!

> **'Intentional activities' are often forgotten when people set their goals.**

Despite their importance, I have found that **intentional activities** are often forgotten when people set their **goals**.

Intentional Activities fall into two categories – the physical actions we take, as well as the energetic actions. A physical action is a tangible **activity** towards the **goal** that can be seen, measured, and/or touched. An energetic action is consciously holding the **goal** in mind, such as meditating and visualizing the **goal** being fulfilled for a specific amount of time each day.

People will say, "I have a **goal**." And really what they have is a wish, or a desire, or a hope.

Here's why…

Without also consciously identifying and scheduling all the **intentional activities** (the commitments of energy) involved in actively achieving the **goal** – there is no generating power to make it happen. As such, it is simply a hope, a wish, a desire that something miraculous will occur and the **goal** will be achieved all by itself.

Of course, every once in awhile, such miracles do occur.

You have probably heard the saying, "where attention goes, energy flows." So, if we focus our attention on planning our **intentional activities**, we are more likely to achieve our **goals**.

Setting Your Goals and Intentional Activities To Fulfill Your *B-All*

Let's return to your list on which you earlier circled three of your top **goals**.

You have already identified your *B-All*.

Now, consider the other two **goals** you have circled. Will the achievement of either of these **goals** help you to fulfill your *B-All*? If your answer is 'yes,' great! Write your *B-All* and that **goal** on a clean sheet of paper.

If your answer is 'no,' great! Take a look at the other **goals** you had written on your sheet, but did not circle. Will the achievement of any of those **goals** help you to fulfill your

B-All? If your answer is 'yes,' then write your *B-All* and one of those **goals** – choose just one – on a clean sheet of paper.

If your answer is still 'no,' then just write your *B-All* on a clean sheet of paper. Then, ask yourself: "what **goal** can I set for myself that would be a first step towards achieving my *B-All?*" Then, write that **goal** on the sheet of paper under your *B-All*.

Next, under the **goal** that you wrote, now write 3 **intentional activities** – meetings, conversations, projects, etc. – to be scheduled and implemented by a certain date and which will bring you closer to fulfilling your **goal**...ultimately supporting you in fulfilling your *B-All* with greater velocity and ease.

These 3 **intentional activities** may take place over the next week, over the next month, or over the next 10 years. It all depends upon the amount of time that you are willing to wait to achieve this first **goal** towards your *B-All*...taking into account that you will have many **goals** to be achieved before your *B-All* is accomplished.

For now, simply make your Plan of 3 **intentional activities** – those activities that will focus your attention on your first **goal** – and write them on your calendar according to a schedule of implementation which feels right and comfortable to you.

Now that you know how we will be using the terms '**goals**' and '**intentions**', here is an example of how **goals** and **intentional activities** generate the energy required to achieve a *B-All* with velocity and speed.

My *B-All* and Goals as an Example

Whether you are an entrepreneur, a member of a sales team, a care-giver, a physician, a lawyer, an entertainer, a massage therapist, a teacher – how ever you use your skills and talents – I acknowledge that you and every other reader of this book will each have your own *B-All* and **goals**, just as each **Chi-To-Be! Master** has their own unique *B-All* and **goals** that they are in the process of achieving. In the following example, I will be sharing my own personal *B-All* and **goals**.

I want to be absolutely clear that these are my **goals**. I am not asking or inviting you to adopt these as your own.

My *B-All* is "to teach thousands of people around the world how to honor and care for their physical, emotional, mental, and energy bodies before I leave this earth."

I have chosen to acquire the certifications and license required to be designated a Doctor of Natural Medicine as the tangible and specific measurement of my #1 Ultimate **Goal**.

Of course, the process of achieving my *B-All* involves the fulfillment of many other important **goals** along the way to achieving my #1 Ultimate **Goal**.

One of my top 3 **goals** I have set to achieve towards my *B-All* is the world-wide implementation of my **Chi-To-Be!** coaching program designed to help every person who has a *B-All* to develop the confidence and skills, as well generate and maintain the inner and outer energy, necessary to achieve that *B-All*. The successful implementation of this coaching program is aligned with my *B-All* because this is an entire program of information to share with others in how to "to honor and care for their physical, emotional, mental, and energy bodies."

Now, here are just a few of the **intentional activities** - the conversations, activities, meetings, and projects, I consciously planned and scheduled at the very beginning of setting this **goal** to ensure the successful fulfillment of implementing my **Chi-To-Be!** coaching program:

· Intentional Activity #1:

Creation of a beta-test group of people who had requested to receive my coaching support. I started with 5 people who wanted to receive the training. The creation of a beta-test group is an example of a physical and tangible **intentional activity** – I was able to measure the number of people in the program, create the tangible materials I would be providing, and plan the schedule of other **intentional activities** that would be involved in the implementation of the coaching program.

· Intentional Activity #2:

Creation of a private website through which I could share information with the beta-test members and they could all communicate with each other to receive support. This was also a physical **intentional activity** – the website could be accessed and seen by the beta-test group.

· Intentional Activity #3:

Conducting group coaching sessions to share the material and provide support to the beta-test group members. Again a physical **intentional activity** – I set dates in advance for these meetings and knew how many people attended them.

· Intentional Activity #4:

Obtaining my license as a Spiritual Healer and my certifications as a Healer Coach, and as an Aromatherapy Coach and Raindrop Technique Practitioner, to increase my knowledge in order to have more information to share through the **Chi-To-Be!** coaching program. Obtaining each license and certification was actually its own <u>physical</u> **intentional activity** with many other **intentional activities** attached, such as registering for the classes required, attending the classes, applying for the certifications and license, and receiving the documentation of the license and certifications.

· Intentional Activity #5:

Scheduling monthly private one-to-one coaching calls with each beta-test group member to provide customized coaching to address their specific issues and blocks to support them in achieving their *B-All* with velocity and ease. A <u>physical</u> **intentional activity** – each one was set on my calendar in advance.

· Intentional Activity #6:

Hosting a weekly internet radio show, called 'AromaWellness in the Palm of Your Hand," as an additional element to the **Chi-To-Be!** coaching program, to share information from various published resources on how to use essential oils… recorded so they can listen over and over again. The show is also made available to the public through pod-casting. This was another <u>physical</u> **intentional activity** requiring other **intentional**

activities, such as arranging for a site to house and record the episodes and researching the information for each episode.

· Intentional Activity #7:

Daily Prayer and Meditation to focus on the successful fulfillment of my **goal**. This involved both an <u>energetic</u> **intentional activity** and a <u>physical</u> one. The <u>energetic</u> was (and still is) the activity of saying my silent prayer and meditation each day. The <u>physical</u> was the **activity** of scheduling on my calendar the actual time each day in which I say my silent prayer and meditation.

· Intentional Activity #8:

Developing a Plan of Promotional Activities to spread the word about the coaching program around the world. Creating the Plan was the <u>physical</u> **intentional activity,** which was generated from many other <u>physical</u> activities, including researching social and traditional media outlets, writing press releases, scheduling interviews, etc.

Each one of these **intentional activities** – and many, many more – generated abundant energy which produced the publication of this book, the accompanying audio series, and the fulfillment of my **goal**: world-wide implementation of my **Chi-To-Be!** coaching program designed to help develop the confidence and skills, as well generate and maintain the inner and outer energy, necessary for every person who has a *B-All* they feel they must achieve!

Unexpected Benefits From Keeping Your Eye On The *B-All*

As I began to construct and implement the beta-test of this coaching program, something wonderful – and unexpected began to happen.

The participants in my beta-test group were telling others about the breakthroughs they were experiencing in their lives as a result of using the tools and strategies provided through the **Chi-To-Be!** coaching program. I soon began receiving numerous requests to participate from the friends of the beta-group members.

And, as I began to receive more and more referrals and requests to participate, it became apparent to me that I would have to create more training materials and more ways of providing support to those I was coaching – since their schedules, geographic locations, and ways of learning became much more diverse.

During one of my prayer and meditation sessions, I received inner guidance that it was time to implement the **intentional activity** of creating a series of recorded audio programs. These audio programs could be accessed any time of day, from anywhere in the world, via computer. This was one way I could reduce the amount of time I spent on delivering the training materials in order to give myself more time to continue my own studies towards my *B-All* of becoming a Doctor of Natural Medicine.

As I continued to focus on how to easily replicate myself over and over again, I also began to consider another **intentional activity** of creating a book from the coaching material.

The book would replace the personalized coaching program, which would free-up even more of my time so that I could continue my own studies.

I was in the process of deciding (an <u>energetic</u> **intentional activity**) whether to issue the material as an e-book to accompany the purchase of the audio programs or to attract a traditional publishing company to publish just the book – when through an amazing and unexpected synchronicity – I met one of the owners of Life Science Publishing. As I was introducing myself to him, I shared about my training program. He asked if I was writing a book about the training program. I said 'yes, it is in development.' To which he immediately replied, "I want that book!"

The same day, he connected me with his two fellow owners and business partners. As I met each one, I **intentionally** asked each of them to tell me what is the 'Most Important Thing' in the world for them?

Why did I ask this question?

I promise you will find out in Chapter 4, Focusing For Energy Generation!

It soon became obvious that what is most important to me in the world – is the same for each of them. What a great foundation on which to build our new relationship!

And, as I **intentionally** shared my vision of the book and the audio series, we **intentionally** began collaborating on other ways to share the information – including the **goal** of developing a world-wide coaching program to be facilitated by Life Science Publishing's coaching staff.

At the time I met the owners, Life Science Publishing had its own **goal** to attract training programs to be implemented by its coaching staff. As it turned out, I attracted Life Science Publishing and Life Science Publishing attracted me because my coaching program was an exact fit...because the principles and tools of the program can be used with success by people in any industry – from all walks of life – in any economic situation!

Now, you may be asking: how will working with Life Science Publishing to publish this book and the accompanying materials support me in achieving my *B-All* with velocity?

I am glad you asked!

Throughout the process of **intentionally** developing my agreement with Life Science Publishing, I kept my eye on my *B-All*.

I now have a new **goal**, which Life Science Publishing and I have jointly set for the success of this project towards the fulfillment of my *B-All*:

The **goal** is now for the coaching program to be facilitated by LSP's coaching staff – and I can again put my full focus on studying and obtaining the necessary certifications towards my doctorate in Natural Medicine.

And, of course, this **goal** has a long list of **intentional activities** planned to ensure its fulfillment, such as researching schools, choosing a school, completing the registration process, etc.

• • • • • • • • • • • **RECAP** • • • • • • • • • • •

1 The place to begin in setting and achieving **goals** with velocity and ease is to identify the #1 **Goal** that you intend to accomplish before you die. That #1 **Goal** is called your *B-All*. Write your *B-All* at the top of a clean sheet of paper.

2 Next, identify all the other top **goals** that must first be accomplished before your *B-All* can be fulfilled.

3 Select one of the top **goals** that you want to achieve first and write this **goal** underneath your *B-All*.

4 Next, identify at least 3 **intentional activities** that you will schedule to complete towards fulfilling the **goal** you selected to fulfill first. Write these 3 **intentional activities** underneath the **goal**. **Intentional activities** provide the generating force or 'chi' that propels us forward to fulfill the **goal**.

5 Schedule these **intentional activities** on your calendar on the dates you want to implement them.

6 As you complete an **intentional activity**, be sure to add another one to the list under your **goal** until that **goal** is completely fulfilled.

7 Once that **goal** is fulfilled, begin with a clean sheet of paper and write the *B-All* at the top. Then, write a new **goal** under your *B-All*. Then, list 3 **intentional activities** you will schedule towards achieving that **goal**. As you complete each

intentional activity, be sure to add another one to the list under your **goal** until that **goal** is fulfilled.

8 Keep repeating #7 until your *B-All* is fulfilled. Then, identify a new *B-All* and begin the process again!

chapter 2
Scheduling For Success

THE 1ST CHI-TO-BE! ENERGY SURGE™

> **surge:**
> Noun: A sudden onrush: *a surge of joy.*
> Verb: To rise and move in a billowing or
> swelling manner; to improve one's
> performance suddenly.
>
> *American Heritage® Dictionary of the English Language*

With your *B-All* established, your top **goals** created, and the
first 3 of your **intentional activities** identified – it's time to now
schedule these **activities** in a way that ensures your success.

Of all the **Chi-To-Be! Energy Surges** you will discover in this
book, SCHEDULING FOR SUCCESS is the foundation of
them all. It is the Surge that supports you in learning to
continually increase the power within you and your business by
capturing and managing with ease all the success that's coming
your way.

This is why SCHEDULING FOR SUCCESS provides the first –
and most important – **Chi-To-Be! Energy Surge!**

How you schedule your **intentional activities** will determine
how much success you achieve from the time and attention you
invest in each one of those **activities**.

Please take a moment to consider if you have ever had this thought:

● ● ● ● ● ● ● ●   [*"There is not enough time in the day for everything I want or have to do!"*]

If so, then you already understand why it is essential for every **activity** – every meeting, every conversation, and every project – to be as productive as possible.

More importantly, you already understand why every **activity** has to be moving you closer to the fulfillment of your ***B-All***... because if it is not moving you closer then you are simply standing still...or worse...moving further away.

At this point, you may want to get your appointment book or open your Calendar feature on your phone or computer. Otherwise, it may be a little more challenging to follow along with me.

Ready?

Good, let's begin.

First, please look at your list of activities for tomorrow.

Is each one of them written on your calendar? Are you sure?

Have you written down the time you plan to wake up? What time you will eat breakfast? What time you will begin each phone call, each appointment, and each and every **intentional activity**?

If not, that's ok. You will have a chance to do it now...in a way that truly supports the fulfillment of your ***B-All***.

Let's begin by looking back at the three **intentional activities** you identified in Chapter 1.

Is there one of these that you would like to take action on tomorrow?

If so, find a time on your calendar for tomorrow that you will take action on this **intentional activity**.

If you feel that none of your three **intentional activities** can be started tomorrow, then please look back at your **goals** and identify one **intentional activity** that you can take and schedule that **activity** on your calendar for tomorrow.

I am now curious how you wrote your **intentional activity** on your calendar.

Most people will put **intentional activities** on their calendar like this: "Phone call with Elliott" or "Research office space". I call this the 'WHAT'...the WHAT will be done. A WHAT is the same as a 'to-do' or a task and it often feels like a chore. And, by scheduling **intentional activities** as tasks, we diminish their importance and our own power to accomplish them.

> **What is much more powerful and energizing instead is to schedule these 'intentional activities' according to the 'WHY'!**

The WHY is our **goal** and our **goal** is the WHY which provides the energy surge to successfully accomplish the **intentional activity**.

For example, **Chi-To-Be! Master** Valerie M. set a **goal** to "completely move into and organize my home office by October 27th" on the way to achieving her *B-All*. On October 18th, she put on her calendar: "to paint most of the remaining white walls in my home (the **intentional activity**) towards completely moving into and organizing my home office by October 27th!" (her **goal**).

And, she accomplished this **intentional activity** right on schedule – because she tied the **activity** to her **goal** on her calendar to remind her of the importance of accomplishing that **activity**!

You may be saying to yourself, *"That sounds so simple."*

I say, "Yes, it is. And, yet most people don't write their **activities** as tied to their **goals** on their calendar and so they forget why it was important to them in the first place. As such, they do not fulfill their **goals** as desired."

Here's another example from one of my coaching clients – a massage therapist – who set an appointment on her calendar with one of her massage clients. She wrote on her calendar the WHAT – 'massage appointment with Janet.'

I asked her: *"Why did you schedule the appointment?"*

She said: *"Because I love doing massage therapy and I make money at it."*

I then asked: *"'doing massage therapy' and 'making money at it' are both* **intentional activities.** *What is the* **goal** *for these* **intentional activities***?"*

She replied: *"To be a Massage Therapist, to be completely booked, and to get paid well for it each and every time."*

I offered this support in reply: *"I recommend that you give power to that* **intention** *by writing the appointment as, 'providing a massage to Janet to receive "x" amount in payment to move towards being a fully booked Massage Therapist and to get paid well for it each and every time.' "*

I then asked her: *"Do you have any idea why I would suggest to you to speak it specifically and write it on your appointment book that specifically?*

She said: *"...so that it becomes a reality?"*

To which I replied: *"Exactly, exactly. You don't just want to have an appointment with Janet. Your* **intentional activity** *is tied to a* **goal***. By writing with the clarity of what you're achieving through that appointment, the energetic power will be transmitted to her back to you. I promise that your appointments will produce more energy and move you closer to the fulfillment of your* **goal** *that much faster.*

As long as you are in the process of achieving this **goal***, you will continue to schedule each and every one of your massage appointments (*intentional activities*) in this same way.*

A Sample Schedule of Success

You may be asking: "Does everything I do in a day have to be an **intentional activity?**"

My answer to this question is: *"Only if you want to ensure that everything you are doing is in alignment and supports the fulfillment of your* **B-All!**

It is just that simple.

Everything you do from the time you wake up to the time you go to sleep…even while you are sleeping…must be in alignment with your *B-All* or you will feel scattered, confused, frustrated and at cross-purposes with yourself. In other words, you will likely feel off-balance.

If you want to keep increasing your personal power and stability, it is important to continue giving your time and attention to **activities** that provide you with energy surges…and those are the **intentional activities** which are taken in harmony with your **goals**.

Chi-To-Be! Master Maria J. upon discovering the importance of 'Scheduling for Success' exclaimed,

> *"Being prepared to handle the success coming my way! Wow! I never realized that I had never done this. My previous success was by the seat of my pants.' I am now looking at my 'Whys' and my 'to do's'! I can see how I can lose my way in a muddled daily existence that steals time and dreams."*

To keep your day and way focused and clear, give yourself 10 minutes now to add to your Calendar all the **intentional activities** that you will be accomplishing tomorrow which support the fulfillment of your **goal**(s) which ultimately will help you achieve your *B-All* with velocity and ease.

If you are a salesperson with a family, and you have multiple **goals** towards your *B-All*, your calendar might look like this:

7:00 a.m.: Wake up and perform my daily meditation ritual towards achieving my **goals** and *B-All* (example: to create and manage my own non-profit foundation to provide funds to those in need).

▶ **7:20 a.m.:** Take a shower towards achieving my **goal** of keeping my body healthy.

▶ **7:30 a.m.:** Take my vitamin and mineral supplements towards achieving my **goal** of keeping my body healthy.

▶ **8:00 a.m.:** Make and eat breakfast with the family towards achieving my **goals** of keeping my body healthy and raising my children to be happy, healthy and successful.

▶ **8:30 a.m.:** Drive the kids to school on time towards achieving my **goal** of raising my children to be happy, healthy and successful

▶ **9:00 a.m.:** Arrive in my office and review my **intentional activities** for the day towards achieving my current monthly **goal** of $20,000 in sales of products.

▶ **9:30 a.m.:** Call to obtain David's commitment to contribute $50.00 towards raising $300.00 for my daughter's class fund-raising project towards my **goal** of raising my children to be happy, healthy and successful.

▶ **10:30 a.m.:** Send David the donation forms to receive his contribution of $50.00 towards raising $300.00 for my daughter's class fund-raising project towards my **goal** of raising my children to be happy, healthy and successful.

▶ **11:00 a.m.:** Meet with Angela over lunch to plan a sales presentation towards my current monthly **goal** of $20,000 in sales of products.

▶ **1:00 p.m.:** Create a plan of **intentional activities** necessary towards ensuring the fulfillment of my current monthly **goal** of $20,000 in sales of products.

▶ **2:30 p.m.:** Review my **intentional activities** planned for tomorrow to ensure I have everything prepared to be successful towards achieving all of my **goals**.

▶ **3:00 p.m.:** Drive to meet with Melissa to receive her product order towards ensuring the fulfillment of my current monthly **goal** of $20,000 in sales of products.

▶ **4:00 p.m.:** Return to office to support current clients and attract new clients as a result of returning phone calls, checking emails, and post on Facebook towards achieving my current monthly **goal** of $20,000 in sales of products.

▶ **5:00 p.m.:** Leave office and drive home towards achieving my **goal** of keeping my body healthy.

▶ **5:30 p.m.:** Prepare a quick, healthy and nutritious dinner for me and the family towards achieving my **goals** of keeping my body healthy and raising my children to be happy, healthy and successful.

    6:00 p.m.: Drive Elizabeth to soccer practice towards achieving my **goal** of raising my children to be happy, healthy and successful.

    8:00 p.m.: Support the children in receiving good grades by reviewing their homework towards achieving my **goal** of raising my children to be happy, healthy and successful.

    9:00 p.m.: Create a pleasant, restful bedtime experience for the kids towards achieving my **goal** of raising my children to be happy, healthy and successful.

    9:30 p.m.: Create a pleasant, restful bedtime preparation experience for me towards achieving my **goal** of keeping my body healthy.

    11:00 p.m.: Begin 7 hours of restful and re-energizing sleep towards achieving all of my **goals** and *B-All.*

Did you notice that every **intentional** appointment, meeting, phone call or other **activity** in this sample schedule had an intended result attached to it – that it was specifically tied to at least one **goal**?

Scheduling Meetings That Fulfill Our Intentions and Goals

The clearer we can be about why we're choosing to schedule an appointment or meeting with another person, the clearer we can be with the other person about what we expect from them during the appointment or meeting, as well.

I confess I learned this lesson the hard way.

> *I used to be the kind of person who would simply hope that a meeting would turn out in my favor.*

I learned quickly that hope was not an empowering force towards the achievement of my **goals**.

Because I now am a Licensed Spiritual Healer, a Certified Aromatherapy Coach, a representative of a line of essential oil products, and the host of a weekly internet radio show about essential oils, I receive numerous requests daily from people wanting to ask me questions about essential oils….which is just one of the many **Energy Surges™** (tools and resources) I share with members of my **Chi-To-Be! Mastery** Coaching Program.

When I first began receiving these requests, I lived in the hope that these people were contacting me because they either wanted to schedule a coaching session with me or to open their own wholesale account to purchase essential oils (another one of my **goals**).

In my excitement, I would automatically set an appointment time as an **intentional activity** with the **intention** of achieving my **goal** of world-wide implementation of my **Chi-To-Be!™** coaching program to help develop the confidence and skills, as well generate and maintain the inner and outer energy, necessary for every person who has a *B-All* they feel they must achieve! (as stated in Chapter 1).

Unfortunately, I did not share my **intention** with these people before meeting with them. As a result, I found that the majority of these people were requesting time with me so they could either promote their own brand of oils or they wanted information about essential oils, but had no interest in providing an energy exchange for my time, expertise and information. Either way, they were not interested in participating in my coaching program.

I finally realized it was my responsibility to share my **goal** with everyone who contacts me – before accepting any requests to schedule an appointment – to ensure that all my **intentional activities** support me in achieving that **goal**.

So now, when someone writes or calls me and asks to "talk about the oils" this is what I reply:

My first question is, *"What would you like to know?"* That helps me to identify their WHY for contacting me.

If they say to me, "Oh, I just want to know more, I'm really fascinated about what you do," I ask if they are already members of my on-line Aromatherapy and Wellness groups on Facebook and/or Meetup.com.

I then go on to say, *"I'd love for you to participate in our group. We have tele-classes, we have in-person gatherings, and there's much information about essential oils on the site for you to access at your convenience at no charge. Then, if you have more specific questions after reviewing the information, I would be most happy to schedule a coaching appointment with you. The first 15 minutes of your coaching session is complimentary to identify your* **goals** *and how essential oils can be of support to you in achieving those* **goals.***"*

I find that the majority of the people who contact me have their questions answered just by visiting the on-line Aromatherapy and Wellness sites. This is a much more productive way for me to be of support to those people while conserving my energy to meet with the people who call me back to schedule a coaching session and who feel they have a *B-All* they must achieve and want to receive my coaching support to develop the confidence and skills, as well generate and maintain the inner and outer energy, necessary to achieve that *B-All*.

There is no ONE right way to schedule your appointments with clarity.

DO IT YOUR WAY, ANY WAY YOU CAN /
THE 2ND CHI-TO-BE! ENERGY SURGE

The principle is to schedule appointments with the clarity which will empower you – propel you – towards your **goal** in the shortest amount of time possible. Then share that clarity with the person(s) you will be meeting to ensure they are willing to participate – or at least explore the possibility of supporting you in achieving your **goals**.

I heard master motivator Zig Ziglar state this truth in the 1990's at an empowerment seminar and it changed my life in that moment.

Up to that point, I was a perfectionist. If I could not do something right the first time…I simply would not even attempt it. I would leave it for someone else to do.

Yet, upon hearing Mr. Ziglar make this amazing, transformative statement: "Anything worth doing is worth doing poorly…the first time," I realized that this was why I had not yet achieved my biggest **goals**.

Because I did not know how to take the first most important step perfectly towards my **goals**, I was allowing myself to stay stuck in not knowing…rather than experimenting, or playing, or researching, or asking for help…anything that would help me to take the first step poorly on my way to perfecting my plan. I feel that Nike's famous line: "Just Do It!," is another way of stating what Zig Ziglar stated.

This is why I say the 2nd **Chi-To-Be Energy Surge** has to be **'DO IT YOUR WAY, ANY WAY YOU CAN!'**

As you practice 'SCHEDULING FOR SUCCESS' using the energy surge of 'DO IT YOUR WAY, ANY WAY YOU CAN!', you will develop greater personal power in gaining clarity about where and how you want to spend your energy, time, money and attention for the greatest return on your investment towards achieving your **goals**.

Chi-To-Be! Masters share their experiences:

 Loralee H.

"Having my **goals** *to keep me on track makes a huge difference for me. With that, I'm able to hold my* **intentions** *for the outcomes of things much better, as well as identify how to become more specific. I've been focused on opening up space in my schedule. For example, I put in a request at my weekday job to cut hours. I've felt rather scrambled and disorganized, so I've spent the afternoon and evening finding homes for things and clearing out stuff. Once I'm done with that it'll be easier for me to move forward with the* **intentions** *and* **goals** *I have for my* **B-All**.

 Valerie M.

"I am noticing that being clear about my **intentions** *is changing the overall outcome of my interactions. It also is changing the initial way I am received when entering into the situation. I find myself having the ability to use fewer words and say more."*

Tara R.

"Now that I know that my **goal** *of being a present and balanced Mother who also strives to master healthy habits is a part of my* **B-All** *(having and continuing to circulate $1 million dollars in the bank to use for helping others in the ways I am guided by God), and my* intentional activities *are related to my* goals, *I am discovering that tasks like folding laundry, working out, or taking the kids to the park FEEL like they are actually helping me fulfill my* **B-All**, *rather than taking me away from that achievement. This is something I have struggled with since becoming a mom. Now I feel whole and grounded, rather than compartmentalized."*

Throughout this book, you will be encouraged to practice and play with utilizing 'SCHEDULING FOR SUCCESS' AND 'DO IT YOUR WAY, ANY WAY YOU CAN' to amp up your power, enthusiasm and joy when using any of the **Chi-To-Be! Energy Surges** still to come!

•••••••••• RECAP ••••••••••

1 SCHEDULING FOR SUCCESS is the first **Chi-To-Be! Energy Surge™** - it forms the foundation for all the Energy Surges to be shared in this book. It is the Surge that supports you in learning to continually increase the power within you by capturing and managing with ease all the success that's coming your way.

2 Every **intentional activity** has to be moving you closer to the fulfillment of your *B-All*...because if it is not moving you closer then you are simply standing still...or worse...moving further away.

3 Tie your **intentional activities** to your **goal** on your Calendar to remind you of the importance of accomplishing those **activities**!

4 Give yourself 10 minutes now to put on your Calendar all the **intentional activities** that you will be accomplishing tomorrow which support the fulfillment of your **goal**(s) which ultimately will help you achieve your *B-All* with velocity and ease.

5 Before scheduling meetings and phone calls, be clear with yourself as to your **intention** and your **goal**. Then, when scheduling the meeting or phone call, share that clarity with the person(s) you will be meeting or calling to ensure they are willing to participate – or at least explore the possibility – of supporting you in achieving your **intentions** and **goals**. If they are not interested in your **intention** and **goal**(s), then why would you want to meet or talk with them any further?

6 As you practice 'SCHEDULING FOR SUCCESS' using the **Energy Surge** of 'DO IT YOUR WAY, ANY WAY YOU CAN!', you will develop greater awareness about how you want to increase your personal power as you gain clarity about where you want to spend your energy, time, money and attention for the greatest return on your investment towards the fulfillment of your **goals**.

chapter 3
Tending to Our Goals

THE 3RD CHI-TO-BE! ENERGY SURGE™

As was mentioned in Chapter 1, to everything there is a season. And, this includes the cycle of fulfillment for our *B-All*.

And, as we explored in Chapter 2, per motivational guru Zig Ziglar: "anything worth doing is worth doing poorly…the first time."

So it stands to reason that there is a cycle of development and mastery that you will move through on your way to fulfilling your *B-All*.

Therefore, it is important to identify what stage of the growth cycle each one of your **goals** towards your *B-All* is in so that you can schedule the most appropriate **intentional activities** for that particular stage in order to achieve all of your **goals** and – ultimately –your *B-All* with velocity and ease.

I like to think of the cycle of achieving my **goals** as the same one I must respect when tending to my garden.

This concept is not new. Many people throughout history have compared the development of a business or project to the life cycle of nature.

What I love about this concept is that it provides me with a consistent energy surge – a reminder that while I focus on achieving my *B-All* – some of my **goals** along the way will be easier to achieve when certain specific conditions are in place.

Stages of Growth

Seeding   **When beginning to create a garden, I know I have to first prepare the ground to accept the *seeds* I will be planting which I intend will flourish.**

You selected the location of your garden in Chapter 1 when you declared your *B-All!*

You began *seeding* the ground in your garden when you identified the **goals** towards your *B-All*.

And, when you scheduled your **intentional activities** in Chapter 2, you began the process of nourishing your **goals** in your *B-All* garden.

During the *Seeding* stage, it is reasonable to expect that it is going to take a certain amount of time and a lot of concentrated energy before we will ever see that first *Sprout* poke out of the ground.

Each **intentional activity** implemented and completed towards your **goal** will require much planning and forethought to ensure that it will produce a result...even a small one. Even more planning and forethought will be required in the *Seeding* stage to ensure the *BLOSSOMING* stage is a long and fruitful one.

I have to be careful to not become frustrated when it feels like I've been **seeding** for a long time and I'm not seeing any *Sprouts*. I know I must continue to water my garden and nourish those **seeds**. Otherwise, I might be giving up five minutes before the miracle – the moment the *Sprout* pokes its head through the soil!

Every experience gained and each lesson learned from each **intentional activity** provides the knowledge necessary of how to plant the next **seed** to produce an even stronger *Sprout*.

Sprouting   **The second stage is the *Sprouting* stage. That's where we start to get the little green tender shoots. But, can we stop fertilizing at that point? No – continuing to tend to the goals planted towards our *B-All* is still just as necessary as it was in the *Seeding* stage.**

Can we stop watering once the **seeds** start producing *Sprouts*?

Of course not! We must continue to plan and implement many **intentional activities** to achieve the **goals** that will support us in bringing our *B-All* to fruition.

There is no fruit yet to enjoy in the *Sprouting* stage. This stage is just as labor, time, and energy intensive as the *Seeding* stage. Just as intensive.

You will notice that there are two primary differences between the *Sprouting* stage and the *Seeding* stage:

1. In the *Sprouting* stage, you are beginning to produce tangible results from your **intentional activities**. One meeting with a potential client/customer is likely to lead

to additional meetings and appointments. You are receiving more requests for information. You are starting to be able to complete your **intentional activities** on time and produce the intended result from those **activities**.

2. In the *Sprouting* stage, you now have a greater number of **intentional activities**. You must keep tilling the soil, and keep talking to the *Sprouting* plants, and remember to keep watering the ones that haven't *Sprouted* yet. This is where it gets a little more difficult than the *Seeding* stage, because the ones that have *Sprouted* need different attention than the ones that haven't sprung yet.

For example, it is possible to make your current customers/clients feel taken for granted at this stage if your **intentional activities** are tied to **goals** that are focused only on attracting new customers/clients.

So, the *Sprouting* stage is the one in which you will have to be sure that you are implementing **intentional activities** to support a variety of different **goals**. You will be tending to a *Sprout* here, *Sprout* there, *Sprout* there, *Sprout* there, until you begin to see flowers *BLOOMING*.

BLOOMING The flowers you see *BLOOMING* are signs your **goal** is being achieved and fulfilled! All the **intentional activities** you implemented in the *Seeding* and *Sprouting* stages have produced an Energy Surge resulting in an entire **goal** being achieved

– a huge *BLOSSOMING* burst of
energy propelling you forward towards the
fulfillment of your *B-All*!

It feels wonderful, it looks beautiful. Yet, this is not time to stop
tending to the **goal**. The **goal** still needs support and attention
to sustain its ability to *BLOOM*. There are still **intentional
activities** to be continuously implemented for that **goal** to
continue to flower.

However, what most people tend to do once they see a **goal**
being achieved is they immediately want to focus on another one
of their **goals**. They take their eye and their energy away from
the *BLOOMING* **goal** and give all of their attention to
intentional activities for a new **goal** to be *seeded*.

Yet, it is essential to the fulfillment of your *B-All* that, during the
BLOOMING stage, you continue to create and implement
intentional activities which will support you in developing and
expanding your abilities to take care of the petunias and the roses
– and even the daffodils – all at the same time...until such time
as the petunias will continue to *BLOOM* on their own...and
then return to a natural **Resting** stage.

Resting

It's to be expected. Every **goal** – once it
flourishes – will also come to a **Resting**
stage. Even after creating the appropriate
intentional activities to sustain the *BLOOM*
on its own for a period of time, the **goal** will
need to **rest** before it can *BLOOM* again
with renewed and vibrant energy!

For example, as Bruce Wilkinson explains in his book, *The Secrets of the Vine: Breaking Through to Abundance,* after BLOSSOMING, a grape vine must be pruned all the way back in order for the grapes to produce a better crop than the last one.

Which, for me, is the answer to that age-old question: Why, when I've done everything right, are there times when it seems like nothing is happening? Or worse – as if I have lost my ability to produce results?

It's because I've reached that fourth stage of letting the **goal** simply **rest** and re-charge itself.

During the **Resting** stage, you will have the time to evaluate what new **intentional activities** the **goal** requires next in order to *BLOOM* again. And, while that **goal** is **Resting**, you can give more attention to other **goals** that are in either the *Seeding* or *Sprouting* stage in order to bring them into *BLOOM*.

Also, as we will explore in depth in Chapter 9, it is important to pro-actively schedule '**rest stops**' for yourself as an ' **intentional activity**' towards completing your **goals** on your way to achieving your *B-All*.

The more **goals** you can keep growing through the cycle of your *B-All* at the same time, the faster you will achieve your *B-All*. Each **goal** – just like different flowers, fruits and vegetables – will *BLOOM* at different times in different ways so you will always have at least one **goal** *BLOOMING* and empowering you to achieve your *B-All*.

A client once asked me, "I am not currently working towards a *B-All*. So would that mean it's in the **Resting** stage?"

My answer is,

> "No. It means you're
> not even in the garden!"

Why Do Some Gardens Grow Lusher Than Others?

As stated above, some **goals** will be easier to achieve when certain specific conditions are in place.

Whether we are building a business or growing another type of **goal**, we must have access to each tool and resource – the sustainable energy – required to grow the **goal** from one stage to the next.

I have coached many clients who asked for my help when they became frustrated that they had not achieved their **goals** by the date they had planned. They were tired, worn-out, and their resources almost depleted by the time they contacted me.

And, in every case, the only issue was that they had not planned to have sufficient resources – the sustainable energy of time, finances, personnel, products, etc. – to allow the **goal** to fully develop though each stage.

This is the primary reason that it is essential to list all the **intentional activities** that will be required to achieve each **goal** – in each stage of growth – before beginning to take action on any these activities towards achieving the **goal**!

The time to know whether or not you will have enough sustainable energy – such as sufficient funding – to keep your energy high during the '*BLOOMING*' stage is not once your

goal is in the '*BLOOMING*' stage. If you want to be sure that your **seeds** will continue to *BLOOM* year after year, then we want to be sure to plan for the *Sprouting*, *BLOOMING*, and **Resting** stages during the *Seeding* stage.

Chi-To-Be! Master Tara R. shares a personal insight she discovered about the *Seeding* stage:

Tara R.

"I feel that 'caring for the soil' in the Seeding stage is also taking care of me in mind, body and spirit. A master gardener friend of mine says about 90% of the work is in the soil preparation. With good strong soil, bountiful crops can be produced."

Remember, your garden – when fully and properly planted with various **goals** – will be in different stages all at the same time.

Each **goal** planted towards achieving your *B-All* and so each one is equally important.

Planning and preparing properly for each stage of growth is what will produce the energy surge to support you in achieving the next stage in the cycle as quickly as possible.

Chi-To-Be! Master Valerie M. states:

Valerie M.

*"I feel one of the **goals** in my B-All garden – to attract 2 new essential oil distributors this month – is in the Sprouting phase. I am nurturing this **goal** with more* intentional activities *– such as more conversations with people who are interested in learning about the oils and scheduling training meetings with my current distributors. I am also learning to identify the weeds, or time-wasters."*

How To Track The Growth Of Your Chi-To-Be! Garden

It is important to keep track on a monthly basis as to how your **Chi-To-Be!** garden is growing according to each **goal**. Identifying the stages will let you know if each **goal** has a sufficient amount of **intentional activities** planned and scheduled to move it into the next stage.

Here's how the **Chi-To-Be! Masters** track their gardens' growth:

 Tara R.

My *B-All* is to have and continue to circulate $1 million dollars in the bank to use for helping others in the ways I am guided by God.

Goal: I complete the Nourishing Your Family Recipes - Volume #1 e-book.

Intentional Activities:

* Meet with graphic designer Monday to finalize copy/links/all sections.
  BLOOMING
* Send potential distributor/publisher teaser edition of the e-book.
  BLOOMING

Goal: Promote my 'Healthy Living' Audio Coaching Series

Intentional Activities:

* Conference with potential distribution partners.
  BLOOMING

- Discuss with fellow Health bloggers syndication for promotion.

Sprouting

Goal: Remain balanced, healthy & loving with my family while caring for the various holiday tasks and financial challenges.

Intentional Activities:

- Implement Holiday "get to do list" and stay within the budget my husband and I have set.

BLOOMING

- Enlist help from my husband and kids to complete seasonal tasks and enjoy completing them together.

BLOOMING

- Create time to exercise three times a week to support my **goal** of practicing and mastering healthy habits.

Seeding

Goal: Experience the 'Chi-To-Be!'™ Mastery Coaching program and respond to the weekly Practice Exercises within the required timeframe.

Intentional Activities:

- Write my input first thing in the a.m. after my morning ritual/and last thing before bed.

Resting *through the holidays*

- Review and complete any unfinished Practice Exercises.

Seeding

Maria J.

My *B-All* is to operate a center called 'The Rainbow Rock Ranch/Resort' in Sedona. This will be a place where people will learn cutting-edge technologies for reversal of the aging process as well as maintenance of optimum health.

Goal: To publish my website:
www.healthyanti-agingwarrior.com

Intentional Activities:

· I set a deadline to complete the tasks to publish the site this month.
· Create time in my schedule to cook and shop for healthy food.
· To conserve energy by getting adequate **rest**.

BLOOMING:

· My current diet of unhealthy foods made me sick and I have been sleeping and tending to my health. I also allowed myself to be distracted by the myriad tasks in my home and all the emails which are piling up. I have consistently completed these steps toward health and energy which will enable me to spend time on website creation.

Goal: To narrow my focus by engaging in only activities which further the creation of my *B-All*.

Intentional Activity:

· To de-clutter my calendar.
Seeding:

I am in the process of remembering to not take things personally, which will create space in my mind. I have been severely challenged in this area this week.

Goal: **Identify ways of reducing spending to create money to purchase a camera for my computer, which I want for updating my website.**

Intentional Activities:

- Design gift certificates to sell during the holidays to increase the revenue I receive from my Massage Business.
- Share space at fund-raiser where I will perform chair massage, sell gift certificates, and give away a free massage as a door prize.

Seeding

Michael T.

My *B-All* is to reach the ultimate state of enlightenment for me and others.

Goal: **To complete the Vitaflex, Mastercleanse and Color Light workshop and obtain another certification.**

Intentional Activity:

- Complete the workshop this month.

Sprouting

Goal: Achieve Mastery in the modalities I facilitate.

Intentional Activity:

- Attending meetings on a regular basis and I have joined the Holistic Chamber of Commerce and attended the first meeting. Schedule demos at a health club.

Sprouting:

- Trained with trainer and head trainer and setting up times to do demos at the club; facilitated a Vitaflex session after a training class for a classmate.

Goal: Create a 3-minute introduction of my services.

Intentional Activity:

- Attended 3 networking meetings and joined two forcing me to give my short presentation.

Sprouting:

- Continue to attend different networking meetings and making 3 phone calls per day.

 # Dez O.

My *B-All* is to successfully open "Screnity Tea House," a spiritually-based tea house where like-minded people may come to relax and find "relief" from day-to-day stress through the serenity of enjoying fresh herbal teas infused with healing energy, crystal energy and essential oils.

Goal: To bring in financial resources towards "Serenity Tea House".

Intentional Activities:

· Develop a new long-distance service for people who live out-of-the-area, who would like to receive my 'Angel Oracle' services.
Seeding

Intentional Activities:

· This month, introduce and promote "Serenity Oracle Reading" telephone or email readings.
Seeding

· Create new classes for 2011 to introduce essential oils in a creative, FUN and educational way, with the possibility of on-line webinar classes, too.
Seeding

· Continue working on new website and blog.
BLOSSOMING

Goal: To remember to honor and support ME by balancing my intentions and taking time to have fun enjoying life with my friends and family.
Intentional Activities:

· To know everything has its Divine Time and Place. There is no such thing as procrastination, it simply means what I am not vibrationally aligned with what I am attempting to do, so I am to stop bucking the system. Instead, do something I am aligned with; the success of what I AM in alignment with will be achieved effortlessly.

BLOSSOMING

- To remember to focus on what the success of each **intention** will FEEL like when it is completed. Let the focus be on the FEELING and let the Universe breathe into life the actual physical manifestation of each of my **intentions**.

BLOSSOMING

 Olivia B.

My ***B-All*** is to ensure my daughter's well being, prosperity, health and strong spiritual connection, while refining my own through core connection to Highest Truth and Deepest Body Consciousness so that we are able to do the work necessary to hold the Earth in balance.

Goal: To make double payments on my Mortgage.

Intentional Activities:

- I will pay off the credit card in two months.
- I intend to reduce all investments for six months.
- I intend to cut any unnecessary expenses.
- I intend to utilize my money management software.

Sprouting:

- I have abided by these **intentions** so the plant is alive and slowly growing into an abundant future. My money management software is still in the **Resting** stage. I intend to wake up that **intentional activity** in two months when there will be fewer bills to enter.

Goal: To participate fully in the 'Chi-To-Be!'™ Coaching program.

Intentional Activity:

- To schedule a conference call with Stacey to discuss my **goals** and **intention** in relation to my *B-All.*

BLOOMING:

- I recognize all the new contacts and appointments that are showing up gracefully. I am looking at my Plan more, changing it according to the issues of improvement that I am currently focused on, and I am very happy with the results I am getting. I feel more organized in my thought process and able to face things head-on instead of stuffing them away for a rainy day.

Goal: To continue Team Building my Young Living® down-line team.

Intentional Activities:

- To be as resourceful as possible in communications by taking the extra step to attach helpful files in information I send.
- To attend events organized by distributors.
- To offer my teaching services.

Seeding, *BLOOMING* and **Resting:**

- New relationships are in the *Seeding* stage, older ones are *BLOOMING* and consistent relationships are **Resting**. This is happening in ways that at first do not seem obvious. I had a breakthrough in identifying unfulfilled agreements and expectations, which is resulting in my up-line connecting more with my team building effort. I am much more optimistic about the courses I am scheduling and the leadership I am taking – all steps towards seeing the larger team working together.

Goal: To spend quality time with my daughter and her father.

Intentional Activities:

- To reunite the family unit for 2 weeks while maintaining clarity of direction and to express myself in a mature friendly manner.
- To be present in each moment with out looking too deep into the past or the future.
- To be respectful and kind as I am with everyone else I love and admire.

Sprouting:

- We had a harmonious 12 hours together in the end of last month and plans are already scheduled for this month although I notice the effort it takes on my part to be present with who he is now, not imagining how he used to be or will be.

 Christina L.

My *B-All* is to win a major live poker tournament with first place being over a million dollars. To use the winnings that I make from winning a major live poker tournament to help people on a grand scale and change the lives of my family and friends.

Goal: To play in the NAPT LA 5k Main Event.

Intentional Activities:

#1: Negotiating the buy-in.

#2: Convincing my backer to give me a shot to win my seat.

Sprouting

• Not only did I win my seat, but I went extremely deep in this tournament, being the last woman standing again, and taking 63rd out of 725 people and cashing in for a little under 10k. This impressed upon my backer that I am a profitable live player, as well as an on-line tournament player. This was a 725k tournament, very close to my ultimate *B-All*.

Goal: Win an FTOPS Event (specifically win a jersey). Last year at this time, I took second. I want to win one to prove that I am capable of winning NOW, with a ton of chips, a major tournament with a huge field that is respected.

Intentional Activities:

#1: Coaching sessions.

#2: Video watching.

#3: Playing poker as much as possible to the best of my abilities.

#4: Asking questions.

#5: Watching online FTOPS final tables as they get 'deep' close to the money.

#6: Securing permission from my backer to qualify to win my seat into the FTOPS Main.

#7: Win my seat into the FTOPS Main.

Seeding
> I intend to have the flower grow by the end of the month.

Goal: Win a small live buy-in tournament this month to up my confidence in building huge stacks, making moves, and being extremely confident in my live game.

Intentional Activities:
> #1: Identify live tournament buy-ins.
> #2: Convince my backer to support me in buying into a few of them after FTOPS is over.
> #3: Trust myself during the tournaments that I know what to do and do it.

Seeding

Goal: To make my house my home so I feel I have a cave to go into to be safe away from the world.

Intentional Activities:
> #1: Clean the carpets.
> #2: Buy a mattress.
> #3: Paint my room.
> #4: Find the perfect bedding.

Sprouting

Loralee H.

My **B-All** is to create a healing center consisting of a wellness package that includes essential oils, bodywork/energy work, coaching, and diet awareness.

Goal: Hold my monthly class.

Intentional Activities:

- Prepare for it by announcing it via emails, Facebook page and other local community websites.
- Do a drawing for someone at the class to experience a Raindrop Technique session.

Seeding:

- I don't have anyone registered to attend this month, yet. The energy has shifted, and my **goal** listed on page 64 is changing, so this is a reflection of that shift.

Goal: Go through my notes and refresh my memory of Raindrop and Neuro-Auricular Techniques.

Intentional Activities:

#1: Invite 4 people to experience a Raindrop or Neuro-Auricular Presentation – Have 1 scheduled, 3 other appointments set to connect with women in my networking group and will invite them when I meet with them.

#2: Send 'thank you' emails after each client appointment. Make sure I have all their emails.

#3: Put a 'session give-away' in the raffle at each networking meeting–did at the first meeting last night.
#4: Do a Bodywork services postcard.
#5: Consult with Stacey to clarify marketing and session procedures–scheduled.
#6: Offer gift certificates for the holidays via emails and in person.

Seeding and *Sprouting*
- Some things in the works, other things on the calendar

**Goal: Build and support my Young Living®
team to grow to the next level of commissions
as 'business builders'.***

Intentional Activities:

#1: Send 'thank you' emails when people order products.
#2: Attract 2 ideal distributors who each open Essential Rewards accounts—I have an appointment set to introduce the oils to someone.
#3: Schedule time to meet with my business builders while in Las Vegas later this month.
#4: Connect with new distributors and support them in starting to use the oils and becoming familiar with the Young Living® website.

Seeding and *Sprouting*
- I opened an account for one new client/distributor. Others are still in process.
*This one took a 180-degree turn, which altered

all my **goals** this month. Revamping and allowing things to surface and gel together. *Seeding*

Goal: Maintain health and self-care.

Intentional Activities:

#1: Continue my workout routine.

#2: Schedule personal time and **rest**.

#3: Observe my diet. Continue eating simply, mostly fruits and veggies.

#4: Spend time with family in Idaho.

BLOOMING:

Doing pretty good here.

An Example of Moving Through The Stages

As stated in Chapter 1, my *B-All* is *"to teach thousands of people around the world how to honor and care for their physical, emotional, mental, and energy bodies before I leave this earth as a Doctor of Natural Medicine."* To accomplish my *B-All*, one of my top **goals** is the world-wide implementation of my **Chi-To-Be! Mastery Coaching** Program designed to help develop the confidence and skills, as well generate and maintain the inner and outer energy, necessary for every person who has a *B-All* they feel they must achieve!

As I mentioned in Chapter 2, I first began to nourish the **goal** by implementing **intentional activities** to attract 5 people to participate in a beta-test of my coaching program. During the *Seeding* stage, it could have required 2 weeks, 2 months or 2 years for me to attract these first 5 coaching participants – it was all dependent upon the number of **intentional activities** I chose to implement and how quickly and with how much **intention**.

The *seeding* **activities** I implemented included creating a **Strategic Attraction Plan™** (see Chapter 4), scheduling informational conversations with potential participants, conducting informational workshops for groups of people, preparing informational materials about the coaching program, attending local networking meetings, as well as a great deal of focused meditation and reflection on the **goal**.

I attracted the first 5 people within 2 months with these activities.

Now, here's a question for you: Once I attracted those 5 people, was my **goal** in the *Sprouting* or *BLOOMING* stage?

The answer is actually, Neither! I was still in the *Seeding* stage.

Before my **goal** could move into the *Sprouting* stage, there were many more **intentional activities** that had to be implemented. First, there was the creation and implementation of **intentional activities** to actually provide the elements of the Coaching Program to these 5 people to determine if the design of the Program would be successful in helping them to achieve their **goals** on the way to achieving their *B-All*. These additional **intentional activities** included scheduling one-on-one and group coaching sessions, writing a workbook of practice exercises, recording audio training sessions, etc. And, these **intentional activities** did prove to be successful in helping these 5 people to achieve their **goals** on the way to achieving their *B-All*. Once that was determined, the **goal** had moved into the *Sprouting* stage. I could see the beginning of *shoots* peeking out through the ground letting me know to keep watering and nurturing my **goal** as it would – ultimately – *BLOOM.*

With this confirmation, I continued to invest time and energy into planning and implementing more **intentional activities** – such as scheduling informational meetings with people who heard about the beta-test and wanted to also participate, scheduling and conducting training **activities** with a larger number of people, writing additional training materials as preparation for the book you are reading, creating a new website for sharing the information world-wide, attending conferences and networking events, developing cross-promotion relationships to spread the word of this coaching program with social media networks, etc. – and then I spontaneously and synchronistically attracted a representative of Life Science Publishing who expressed interest in producing and distributing my book and other training materials.

Was my **goal** *BLOOMING* at that point? No, not yet!

My **goal** was in a very full stage of *Sprouting.* The *shoots* were growing taller and taller. I was coaching a larger number of people. I was receiving a greater amount of financial compensation. My website was in development. I was receiving interest in my program from people outside of the United States.

Yet, the **goal** *still required more nourishment – continued time and effort focused on implementing the* **intentional activities** *already planned to address and respond to each one of the* **shoots** *– in order for them to become* **BLOOMING** *flowers and fruit.*

I was not yet at the stage of "world-wide implementation" of the coaching program.

As busy as I was attending to each one of the *shoots* I was expecting to develop, I now had a new *seed* to nurture – if I chose to do so.

This was the *seed* of developing an Agreement with Life Science Publishing which could possibly support me in achieving my **goal** with even greater velocity and ease than I had previously envisioned. This ultimately would make it possible for me to achieve my *B-All* even faster!

With the **intention** that such an Agreement must be an energy booster to propel me forward on my path towards achieving my *B-All*, I did choose to also plan, schedule and implement more **intentional activities** to grow the new *seed* into a *Sprout*.

These **activities** included phone calls with the representatives of Life Science Publishing to plan and coordinate our **activities** towards achieving our mutual *B-All* and **goals**, as well as conversations with lawyers, reviewing contracts and writing a first draft of the book.

As I am sure you can imagine, during the *Sprouting* stage, I relied heavily on the **Chi-To-Be! Energy Surge #2: 'DO IT YOUR WAY, ANY WAY YOU CAN!'**(Chapter 2) to keep a sense of balance in my life while keeping my eye on my *B-All*.

And, as stated earlier in this Chapter, and as demonstrated by this example, the *Sprouting* stage is very labor-intensive and requires energy, patience and passion – as well as a strong commitment – to bring all the *Sprouting shoots* into the fullness of life. The good news is, just like a rose bush given the proper amount of sun, shade, water and nourishment, the reward will be a long *BLOSSOMING* stage!

For my **goal**, the buds began appearing once the contract with Life Science Publishing was signed and the first draft of this book was accepted. In order to bring these first buds into full *BLOOM*, there were new **intentional activities** to be scheduled and implemented…while continuing to implement all the coaching program **activities** required in support of the participants I had already attracted….as well as all the **intentional activities** for all of my other **goals**!

These new **activities** included enlisting the participation of the **Chi-To-Be! Masters** to share their experiences in this book, requesting approvals and permissions from publishers of other books mentioned in this book, requesting and receiving bids from production companies to produce the new audio program, forming an editorial board to review the book manuscript, numerous re-writes to the book manuscript based on the editorial board's feedback, recording the audio program, reviewing and approving a book cover design, attracting an event production assistant, attracting a social media expert, writing copy for the website, writing and distributing press releases, developing a larger number of cross-promotion relationships, creating and implementing launch events to share the information around the world, accepting and conducting interviews with media outlets, responding to a larger number of requests for information, posting more messages on social networking sites, paying closer attention to getting sufficient **rest** and eating nutritiously to sustain my health, meditating daily, and the list of **intentional activities** continues to grow while my **goal** is in full *BLOOM*.

I stated above that, just like a rose bush given the proper amount of sun, shade, water and nourishment, the reward will be a long

BLOSSOMING stage! The reward can only be obtained, however, if sufficient resources are available to sustain this stage of growth. This is why I mentioned earlier the importance of planning for these resources back in the *Seeding* stage.

Why the Blooming Stage Requires the Most Energy

People often ask me how I am able to accomplish so much in such a short amount of time. My answer is always that I use all of the **Energy Surges** I am sharing with you in this book.

Of all of these, 'Scheduling For Success' and 'Tending To Our Goals' are the two that propel me forward with velocity towards my **goals**...especially when my **goals** reach the *BLOSSOMING* stage.

In my years as a coach, I've found that most people moving through the stages for the first time are unprepared to sustain a long *BLOSSOMING* period. The primary reason is that they have an unrealistic expectation that everything will be easier and run smoothly when their **goal** is in full *BLOOM*. They expect this stage to be the one in which they can relax and reap the benefits. And, yes, while there are many delicious and fulfilling benefits and rewards – such as larger amounts of financial compensation, a greater number of clients/customers, time to take short **rest stops**, more partnerships, more fame, etc. – each one of these rewards will produce **intentional activities** in greater abundance, as well.

In the *BLOOMING* stage, there will be more **activities** to create and to implement, new relationships to attract, and financial expenditures required that were not required previously.

In this stage, if I attempt to undertake too many **intentional activities** by myself, I will deplete my energy.

> *There are just so many hours in the day, so more time and energy given to one* **intentional activity** *means that the time and energy given to others may be diminished and/or halted.*

For example, during the **Seeding** and **Sprouting** stages of my **goal** I could manage responding to correspondence and other **intentional activities** by myself. As the coaching program became known world-wide, it attracted more attention, so did the amount of correspondence and other **intentional activities** which require a response. I began to notice that I was on the computer for longer periods of time each day responding to inquiries and spending less time on other **activities** that were equally important to the success of this **goal** and my other **goals**.

In order to keep my time, energy and focus on the **intentional activities** that only I can do and which provide me with the energy to move forward – such as spending time with my family, eating nutritiously, getting sufficient sleep, keeping my commitment to my Agreements with my publisher, providing coaching support – I chose to hire an assistant to support me in handling these **activities** with ease.

Other relationships that are required to assist me in addressing all the aspects of my abundant **goal** are a website developer, a social media expert, an event coordinator, a bookkeeper just to name a few.

At the beginning of the *BLOOMING* stage, there will likely be more money being expended than received. This was exactly the case for me. So, it is essential that I had planned for the added expense of hiring an assistant and these other relationships and secured the funds for them while I was still in the *Seeding* stage.

I invite you to take a moment now to consider what relationships you will want to attract to support you when your **goal** is in full *BLOOM*.

How will I know when my goal is in the Resting stage?
At this point in the *BLOOMING* stage, you may be feeling in need of a **rest**. However, your **goal** is not! In Chapter 9, we'll explore how to take short **rest stops** to re-charge your energy while your **goal** is still *BLOOMING*.

While in the *BLOOMING* stage, a few of the **intentional activities** that had produced results previously may not be as productive or as necessary to implement as they were at the beginning of the stage. For example, once a website has been designed, it's not likely that every page will require edits or additions on a regular basis. The amount of energy that was required and dedicated to designing the web site can now be diminished…or even be at **rest** for awhile. Or, once an event has been created and produced, there may only be a few follow-up **activities** still requiring attention; the majority of the energy is now at **rest** and available to other **intentional activities**.

Or, if you are a parent and your **intentional activity** is to potty-train your child towards the **goal** of supporting your child in his developmental growth, once your child is completely potty-trained, the energy expended on that **activity** is now at **rest** and available to be used for implementing some other aspect of the **goal**, such as teaching him how to read.

Some **intentional activities** may be seasonal – better suited to producing results during certain times of the year – it's best to let the energy given to these **activities 'rest'** at other times.

If while in the *BLOOMING* stage, I take my attention and energy away from the **goal** completely in order to give the attention to a different **goal**, and the first **goal** does not continue to produce *BLOSSOMS*, then we could say the first **goal** was in the **Resting** stage waiting for me to give it additional attention to produce it's next *BLOSSOMING* cycle. The caution here is I must be sure that I tended the first **goal** so well that it has grown strong roots from which to easily produce another harvest once I return to give it more attention.

And, the closer I come to fulfilling my *B-All*, more and more of the **goals** I set for myself to achieve along the way will have been accomplished and more energy is now available for me to use as I focus even more fully on my Ultimate **Goal**.

Until that time, my **goals** will require consistent and focused attention – each **intentional activity** requiring much expended energy. I will be utilizing each of the **Chi-To-Be! Energy Surges** to be discussed in the remaining chapters to keep myself energized, strong and powerful all the way to the fulfillment of my *B-All*!

**Another Example of Tracking The Stages Provided by
Chi-To-Be! Master**

 Loralee H.

My *B-All* is to change the world and people's lives in a positive and influential way and thus be financially successful and extremely happy.

My first goal: I would like to continue to build a stronger relationship with my backer and work out a deal with him where I have a separate live and online backing deal and he wants to put me in major live tournaments and we come to an agreement that is mutually beneficial.

Intentional Activities

· My backer and I have profited around $14,000 each since he has been backing me. Once we each cash out $50,000, he will give me a separate live and online deal, and I will be playing for 55% of myself, instead of 50%.

· I am beginning to produce results and playing as much as I can in order to get better, gain more experience, and thus achieve my **goal** to reach the *BLOOMING* and **Resting** stage. This **goal** is in the *Sprouting* stage.

My second goal: Get my living situation 100% straightened out. Have my former roommate move out; get a thorough cleaning of my apartment, including organizing everything.

Intentional Activities:

- I have and will thoroughly clean and straighten out all of the negative energy. It will be in the **Resting** stage November 1, once my new roommate moves in and we get 100% situated and I move out the last of the other person's things.
- My apartment is 90% organized. I will finish up the last bits of organizing and have a great apartment, with my perfect roommate! This **goal** is in the *BLOOMING* stage.

My third goal: I intend to become financially stable and have a constant income. I intend to profit at least $20,000 for both my backer and I this month and continue to have success online, winning at least one major; thus reaching the goal of my backer, and each cashing out $50,000 so he will allow me to play any live tournaments.

Intentional Activities:

- I have profited a little less than the amount I have written; and, there is still time to achieve my **goal** when I play Sunday.
- I won a highly respected tournament, which is regarded as one of the toughest tournaments online.
- I am continuing to work hard and keep my *B-All* and **goal** in my mind every time when I play.
- I have also been using essential oils constantly to aid me in my success and help me to keep a positive attitude when playing. This **goal** is in the *Sprouting* stage.

•••••••••• RECAP ••••••••••

1 You will move through a growth cycle of development and mastery on your way to fulfilling your *B-All*.

2 It is important to identify what stage of the cycle each of your **goals** towards your *B-All* is in so that you can schedule the most appropriate **intentional activities** for that particular stage in order to achieve your **goals** and your *B-All* with velocity and ease.

3 The 4 stages of **goal** achievement are similar to the stages of the growth of a garden:

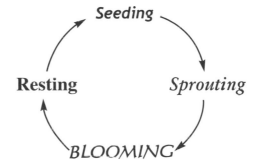

Seeding

Resting   *Sprouting*

BLOOMING

4 During the *Seeding* stage, it is reasonable to expect that it is going to take a certain amount of time and a lot of concentrated energy before we will ever see that first *Sprout*. Each **intentional activity** implemented and completed towards your **goal** will require much planning and fore-thought to ensure that it will produce a result…even a small one. This is also the stage in which it is important to plan for acquiring the resources required during the *Sprouting* and *BLOOMING* stages.

5 In the *Sprouting* stage, you are beginning to produce tangible results from your **intentional activities**. This is the stage where you will also have to be sure that you are implementing **intentional activities** to support a variety of different **goals**.

6 In the *BLOOMING* stage, all the **intentional activities** you implemented in the *Seeding* and *Sprouting* stages have produced an energy surge resulting in an entire **goal** being achieved – a huge energy surge forward to the next stage of the cycle of your *B-All*!

7 A **goal**, even after creating the appropriate **intentional activities** to sustain the *BLOOM* on its own for a period of time, may need to **rest** before it can *BLOOM* again with renewed and vibrant energy!

8 The more **goals** you can keep growing through the cycle towards your *B-All* at the same time, the faster you will achieve your *B-All*.

9 Utilize each of the **Chi-To-Be! Energy Surges** to be discussed in the remaining chapters to keep your energy strong and powerful throughout each of the growth stages to ensure you are able to fulfill your *B-All* with velocity and ease!

chapter 4
Focusing For Energy Generation

4TH CHI-TO-BE! ENERGY SURGE™

The concept of 'focusing for energy generation'...is about
staying focused on the people who can help us to achieve our
goal(s) faster because they either share our same **goal**(s) or they
can support us in some other way.

Back in 1996, while helping one of my clients to identify key
groups of influential people on which she could focus her
intentional activities, she asked me how she would "find" these
people since she had just started her business and did not already
know these types of people.

At the time, I already had more than 16 years of experience as an
advertising account executive and then a corporate marketing
executive for Budget Rent a Car Corporation and Federal
Express Corporation. It would have been easy for me to simply
create the marketing plan for her business.

However, I was working with a small business owner and I knew
that it was more important for her to learn how to create her own
plan of action – her own list of **intentional activities** towards
her **goals** – to generate her own energetic power.

The challenge (**goal**) for me in that moment was how to teach
her in just one hour all the marketing knowledge that I had
learned over 16 years.

As I meditated on how to achieve this **goal**, I received inspiration in the form of a simple formula that would make it easy for my client to understand how to 'attract' key groups of people to her business.

The formula is based on the Law of Attraction – like attracts like – on the level of energetic frequencies or vibrations.

When using the power of the Law of Attraction, it is not necessary to 'find' key groups of people. Instead, we easily draw to us other people whose energetic vibration is the same as ours.

This is why it is so important to keep our energetic vibrations at a high level if we intend to attract people who have the energy to help us achieve our **goals**…and ultimately our *B-All*!

ATTRACTING IS AN INTENTIONAL ACTIVITY

I proved this theory to myself over the next five years by teaching all of my clients how to use the formula.

I called the formula **'The Strategic Attraction Planning Process'™** and I even used it to attract a business partner/ co-author, a literary agent, and a publisher who supported me in 2001 in achieving my **goal** of writing and publishing *'Attracting Perfect Customers…The Power of Strategic Synchronicity,'*(1) in which the formula was featured.

The book was released to rave reviews. Here's just two:

——●—●——●——

"By connecting with the power of Strategic Synchronicity, your work will give you a much higher rate of return in satisfaction, productivity, and profitability. You will be

inspired, encouraged, and delighted by how quickly this process works in attracting your most perfect customers."
— Jack Canfield, co-author of the #1 New York Times Bestseller 'Chicken Soup for the Soul®' series

———•—•——•———

"This is an incredibly insightful book with amazingly practical applications. The power of attraction in business is a powerful concept that anyone can use to grow faster and with greater predictability. Wow!" — Brian Tracy, author of 'The 100 Absolutely Unbreakable Laws of Business Success' and 'The 21 Success Secrets of Self-Made Millionaires"

Since its release in 2001, 'Attracting Perfect Customers...The Power of Strategic Synchronicity,' has been re-printed numerous times and translated into a variety of languages. **'The Strategic Attraction Planning Process'™** has been proven to work around the world and for every type of business imaginable.

After years of creating my own Plans, I now realize that **'The Strategic Attraction Planning Process'™** is a powerful **intentional activity** that helps me to focus for energy generation and attract the most influential people who can support me in achieving my **goal(s)** with power and ease.

This is why I enjoy sharing the book and the Process with others.

Chi-To-Be! Master Sandra Lee Schubert created her own **Strategic Attraction Plan™** and shares:

"From here on, I will thrive. I see myself asking better questions in a situation, planning my day around my **Strategic Attraction Plan™** *rather then wishful thinking, creating my* **goals** *around*

a solid plan of who I am and what I want; creating a life that brings in the people, places and things that support the life I want to live!"

You may wish to read *'Attracting Perfect Customers...The Power of Strategic Synchronicity,'* as an **intentional activity** towards any and all of your **Goals** to understand the 'how' and 'why' this Process works so well.

Later in this chapter, I will guide you through a simple process for creating your own **Strategic Attraction Plan™**. I have been further refining the Process for myself over the past 6 years. The simplified version provided in this chapter is my refinement of the original formula featured in *'Attracting Perfect Customers...The Power of Strategic Synchronicity.'*[1]

To assist you in identifying groups of people whom you may wish to focus on to leverage your time, energy and resources, a few of the **Chi-To-Be! Masters** have offered to share the groups that they are attracting:

 Corey S.

B-All: To create my successful entertainment company.
Goal: Start recording my own music and begin to attract like minds.

Most Influential People Right Now:
Entertainment Business Builders

Sandra S.

B-All: I am known for my great work that inspires and motivates people to create their own great work and live an inspired life.
Goal: Book two clients into my "The Business Monthly Maintenance' package.

Most Influential People Right Now:
"Great Work" Clients

 Lauren K.

B-All: To change the world and people's lives in a positive and influential way and thus be financially successful and extremely happy.
Goal: Work out a mutually-beneficial deal with my backer where I have a separate live and online backing deal and he backs me to play in major live tournaments.

Most Influential People Right Now:
A Poker Sponsor

 Michael T.

B-All: To reach the ultimate state of enlightenment for me and others.
Goal: To build financial freedom in the development of my Young Living® business.

Most Influential People Right Now:
Young Living® Distributors

DeZ O.

B-All: To create my "Serenity Tea House"
Goal: Create my first Blog site.

Most Influential People Right Now:
Serenity Living Wellness clients

What Comes Before The Plan

In order to create your **Strategic Attraction Plan™**, you must first identify the groups of people who will be most influential in helping you to achieve your **goals** as quickly as possible.

To begin, pick one of the three **goals** that you created in Chapter 1 that you will accomplish in order to achieve your ***B-All***. It does not matter which one you decide to pick…any one of the three will do.

Now, think about all the people that will be involved in the fulfillment of that **goal**.

Perhaps you will need clients to help you fulfill the **goal**. You may need investors or backers to fulfill the **goal**. You may require a business partner to help you achieve the **goal**.

Perhaps you may need all of these types of people to help you achieve your **goal**. If so, identify the ONE type of person or group of people that is/are the most important group of people for you to attract right now.

For inspiration, take another look at the list of **Chi-To-Be! Masters** who identified the ONE type of person or group of people that will help them achieve their **goals** as quickly as possible.

Once you have identified your most important type of person or group of people, you are ready to create your own **Strategic Attraction Plan™**:

Begin with a clean sheet of paper and fold it in half. This will give you 4 sides on which to write your Plan.

1. Choose which side will be Side #1. At the top of Side #1, write:

The qualities of my perfect _____,

and fill in the blank with the type of person or group of people you identified above.

Consider all the qualities and characteristics that this type of person or group of people will all demonstrate in order to help you achieve your **goals**. How will you want them to act in relationship to you and others? What actions will you want them to take to support you? What will you want them to purchase? What character traits do you want them to possess? Write all these descriptions as a list on Side #1 under the title.

One way to begin to create this list is to use a role model that you already know. They may be a client, a friend or a family member. This is the person that you enjoy being around the most. This person may be a part of your life right now or you may have known them in the past. Allow yourself the opportunity to think about this person, and remember what you enjoy(ed) about them so much. Remember, the quality of your interactions with this person. Describe this person to yourself in all the ways that they were a perfect fit for you to have in your life. Then, write all those qualities on Side #1 under the title.

For example, if you remember that you like that they always smiled, write down 'they always smile.' If you found that they said 'thank you' often, write that down. If you liked the way they dressed, write that down. If they happened to be a customer, and they paid you what you wanted them to pay you, write that down. If they were a teacher and you liked the way they shared information with you, write that down. Write down every positive quality that you can think about this particular person. List at least 10 qualities.

Remember, this person is serving as a role model for the type of person you are intending to attract. However, they probably won't have all the qualities you want to attract. If you want to attract a book publisher and your role model does not have book publishing experience, then you will be missing some important qualities from your list. So now look at the list on Side #1 and see what qualities are missing. What other important qualities would you add to describe the type of person or group of people who are the most important in helping you achieve your **goal(s)**?

If you feel stuck, you may wish to turn now to the Appendix to view the Sample Attraction Plan. Feel free to take any of the qualities you see listed on the Plan and add them to yours – if these are qualities that describe the type of people who are most important to you to attract.

2. Let's flip over to Side #2. At the Top of Side #2, please write:

"What makes me tick?"

Begin by answering this question: "What is the most important thing in the world to you?" What is your answer? Think about it, but don't write it down on Side #2 just yet.

Now, describe what "the MOST important thing" in the world represents to you – or said another way, why is it so important to you? Take a moment to consider that question. Don't write anything on Side #2 yet.

Once you have that answer, ask yourself 'what does this represent to me" or "why is it important to me?" Continue to ask these questions of yourself without writing anything down.

$$\bullet \ \bullet \ \bullet \ \bullet \ \bullet \ \bullet \ \bullet \ \bullet \quad \left[\begin{array}{l} \textit{Each time you arrive at a new answer,} \\ \textit{ask again 'what does this represent to} \\ \textit{me?" or "why is this important to me?"} \end{array} \right]$$

Please know that as you go through this series of questions, every answer is absolutely the right answer. With each question, you are taking yourself to higher and higher vibrations of the same answer.

At a certain point, you will find that the question brings you repeatedly back to the same answer. Until you reach that point, be sure to let the process unfold; stay with it. Maybe you have to ask yourself seven times, what does that represent?

Why is that so important?

When you get to the final answer – the answer to which you keep returning – consider this: if it was no longer possible for you to experience what is most important to you – would you want to get out of bed tomorrow morning?

For example, let's say that you said that the most important thing to you is family, and family represents security, caring, comfort to you.

Next, you said that 'security, caring, and comfort' represent 'love,' and 'love' represents to you 'love.' In other words, you simply can not think of any other way to describe 'love' except as 'love.'

That's the point when you've reached the end of the questioning. So, now the question becomes, "if love was never again possible to experience, starting tomorrow morning when you woke up, would you want to get out of bed?"

If the thought of losing what is most important in the world to you (Love) brings you to tears, or a sense of hopelessness, or a sense of "what's the point?" then you would know that what makes you tick is 'love'…that 'love' is the most important thing in the world to you.

However, if you've gotten to the final answer and you say to yourself, "Well, yeah, I could still get up in the morning," then I would say that you probably have not yet reached your absolute final answer. Continue the exercise until you know you have reached that final answer.

That final answer is the answer that you will write down on Side #2.

If you are having difficulty in getting to the final answer, you may wish to use the 5 questions provided on page 76 of *"Attracting Perfect Customers…the Power of Strategic Synchronicity."*[1]

Question One:
   "Why do you get out of bed in the morning?"

Question Two:
   "Who is the most important person to you in the world?"

Question Three:
"What is most important to you in the world?"

Question Four:
"What do you want to achieve before you leave this world?"

Question Five:
"What do you really love about your life?"

These questions are all designed to help you get to that final, ultimate answer of what truly makes you tick.

You may say, well what does this have to do with my **goal** and the most influential people I need to attract to achieve my **goal**?

Here's the only reason: the Law of Attraction works on the principle that 'like attracts like.'

Your answer to 'what makes you tick' is what gives meaning to your life. It is as essential to your life as the blood that courses through your veins. That answer goes hand-in-hand with your *B-All*! In fact, it is the reason why you have committed to fulfilling your *B-All*

Most importantly, it is what makes you so attractive to certain people…the people who will be most influential in helping you to achieve your **goals**.

They will be attracted to help you because their answer to the question 'what makes you tick?' will be the same as yours! When you are connected to your answer to 'what makes you tick?' you will be able to draw these people to you …synchronistically!

It will happen in the same way that you easily attracted all the people with whom you are already enjoy close, loving and supportive friendships (which may or may not include the family into which you were born).

Take a moment to again think about the person that you used as the model for Side #1 – the one that you most enjoyed having in your life – consider what they would answer to the question 'what makes you tick?' I will not be surprised to learn their answer is the same as yours.

I've been teaching the **Strategic Attraction Planning Process**™ for 16 years to people from around the world. And, I have yet to meet one person who told me that the answers were different.

Now that you have identified your answer to 'what makes you tick?', you are ready to create Side #3.

3. At the top of Side #3, write:

What Do I Want My Perfect _____ (Fill-In-The Blank) To Expect of Me?

The vast majority of us were taught to put less attention on ourselves and more on others. As such, we have become masters at adapting ourselves to the needs of others.

In the **Strategic Attraction Planning Process**™, the focus and attention is shifted back to what we want! The shift occurs on Side #3.

On Side #3, it's OK to be selfish, because in being selfish we are always keeping our eye on the *B-All*. We know that to achieve all of our **goals**, we must be clear in identifying which **intentional activities** will receive our energy and attention.

No one else knows better than we do what we want others to expect of us – how we want them to expect us to behave, what activities and projects we will accomplish, what **goals** we intend to achieve.

On Side #3, list your answers to the question at the top of Side #3 with these other questions in mind:

1. How do you want people to see and perceive your actions?

2. What qualities do you want to demonstrate in your interactions with others?

3. What is your *B-All* ?

4. What are the **goals** you expect yourself to achieve before your *B-All* can be fulfilled?

5. What characteristics from Side #1 do you also want people to expect of you?

Your list can be as long as you wish. I suggest beginning Side #3 by listing at least 15 items. To assist you in thinking of items to add to your Side #3, you may wish to use some of the items that I and the **Chi-To-Be! Masters** have listed on our Plans…

(Bold items = items that are not yet
achieved/accomplished)

Stacey's Side #3 Sample List
B-All:
– **I am a Doctor of Natural Medicine**
Qualities:
  – I am trustworthy.
  – I am generous in spirit.
  – I am dependable.
  – I believe that miracles occur in my life every day.
  – I treat myself and others with respect.
  – I enjoy collaborating and co-creating with others in ways
     that support us all to achieve our *B-All*.
Goals:
– **I am licensed and certified as a Doctor of Natural
  Medicine.**
– **I have successfully achieved world-wide.
  implementation of my Chi-To-Be! coaching program**
– **I am proficient at email, Facebook and Twitter.**
– **I always receive an equal or greater exchange of
  energy for sharing my gifts with others.**
– **I am easily and fully developing the programs and
  projects of Chi-To-Be!, LLC.**
– **I am receiving and then depositing $xxx,000.00+ of
  revenues each month into my bank account for the
  next 50+ years from donations, sales and royalties of
  programs and projects I produce and/or facilitate,
  and these funds are always available to me for use as
  I desire.**
– **I take a 4-week vacation in Australia with
  my husband.**

Intentional Activities:

– I reply to requests when it is perfect for me to do so.

– I pray and meditate every morning and night.

– I schedule 3 hours each day for coaching appointments with my clients.

– I add more items to my **Strategic Attraction Plan™** every day.

– **I schedule 1 hour each day to add to my knowledge of how to maintain my own wellness.**

Chi-To-Be! Master Michael T. Sample Side #3

B-All:

– **I reach the ultimate state of enlightenment for me and others.**

Qualities:

– I am passionate about my products and services.

– **I am impeccable with my word.**

Goals:

– **I build financial freedom in the development of my Young Living® business.**

– **I am designing an environment that pulls me forward.**

– **I pull in $xxxx.00 a month in 3 months, $xxxx.00 a month in 6 months, and $xx,xxx.00 a month in a year.**

Intentional Activities:

– I am taking a happy, healthy, wealthy **intentional activity goal** action step everyday to make it a habit.

– **I am knocking off my tolerations list one at a time to free my energy.**

Chi-To-Be! Master Corey S. Sample Side #3
B-All:
- I create my successful entertainment company which brings a high level of artistry back into the entertainment industry.

Qualities:
- I am present.
- I stay connected with friends and family.
- I ask questions when I need clarity.
- I am punctual.
- I do what I can when I can and am comfortable with that.

Goals:
- I take a nature walk/ hike once per week.
- I am recording my own music .
- I am familiar with products that I am referring to others.
- I attract like minds.
- I own a MacBook Pro by 2011.

Intentional Activities:
- I am learning Pro tools.
- I am recording.
- I am performing.
- I do rejoice.
- I acknowledge my accomplishments.
- I ask for support when I feel it is needed.
- I read 2 books per month.
- I meditate daily.
- I provide accurate educational information to others.
- I work on music at least 2 hrs daily.
- I am learning healing methods.

Chi-To-Be! Master Sandra S. Sample Side #3

B-All:
- I am known for my great work that inspires and motivates people to create their own great work and live an inspired life.

Qualities:
- I actively follow my own successful social media strategy by interacting with friends, family, colleagues, clients & potential customers across all social networks I use.
- I am proficient at email, Facebook & Twitter & other technologies.
- I have a prosperity & gratitude mindset.
- I do what it takes to breakthrough any breakdowns I encounter on the way to achieving my own *B-All.*
- I am an attractor, radiating love & light drawing goodness, love, & riches to me.

Goals:
- I book two clients into my 'The Business Monthly Maintenance' package.
- I develop ebooks & courses around my "How to Start a Internet Radio Show," Social Media Coaching, writing ecourse, and other Great Work programs I develop.
- I launch my own small press publishing company producing my own best selling books and providing an imprint for others to publish their own books.
- I have a stable & happy home life.
- I easily receive $x000.00+/month in commissions paid to me from affiliate for sales of their products.
- I easily receive $xx,000+/year in donations received for my Spiritual Healing Coaching facilitation services.
- I have attracted customers who live in the U.S., Canada, Australia, Mexico, South America, &

Europe, Asia, Africa & other areas that are
accessible easily by phone or internet.
- I easily & effortlessly pay all my monthly, quarterly,
yearly bills on the dates requested & in full.

Intentional Activities:
- I practice my morning & evening ritual every day.
- I am actively building my business through planning
& implementation of a successful marketing
strategy.
- I use my social media time effectively by scheduling
updates via hootsuite or a similar platform.
- I spend at least 1 hour, in increments, throughout the
day in following up on email & social media for
myself. I keep track of my clients' social media
needs 3-5 hours a day, 5 days a week, utilizing virtual
assistants & at least one hour of my time for gold
member clients.
- I am available during the hours of 8 PM to 10 PM
est., Monday through Friday or through convenient
appointment, arranging appointments through
online applications such as tungle.me, Google
calendar & my date book.

Welcome back. So now you've got at least fifteen items that you
want people to expect of you.

Next, take a look at your list of the *Qualities* that you want to
demonstrate, the **goals** you want to achieve, and the **intentional
activities** you are in the process of completing and highlight or
bold each one of the **goals** and **intentional activities** that you
have not yet completed and/or fulfilled. These are the **goals**
and **intentional activities** which you're still working towards
completing; you're still "in process." They may even be **goals**
for the future that haven't manifested yet, like a revenue **goal**. It

doesn't matter if you have one item or a hundred items that are highlighted or in **bold**.

For example, you can see that I have listed – **I am easily and fully developing all the programs and projects of Chi-To-Be!, LLC.**

One of the groups of people I am attracting are people who want to participate in the **Chi-To-Be! Mastery Program.** I do want these people to expect that I am developing more programs and projects. Since these programs and projects are still in development, this **goal** is not yet complete or fulfilled. This is why I have listed it in **bold**.

Once you've highlighted or put in **bold** the items that are still in process or development, we'll move on to Side #4.

4. At the top of Side #4, please Write:

> *"What I Am in the Process of Improving to be More Attractive!"*

For this side, I'm actually going to give you the answer too!

How easy is that?!

Here's the answer: Please write it just like this, *"Anything and everything that is highlighted or in* **bold** *on Side #3."*

Now you may say to me, "But Stacey, I'm working on many more things than just those items on Side #3. In fact, my 'to do' list is ten times as long as the list on Side #3."

Here's my answer: Take a look at your 'to do' list and first identify the items on your 'to do' list that you really want to do.

These are likely to be **intentional activities** towards a specific **goal**. If so, then be sure to add these items to Side #3, too. And, since you have not accomplished them yet, be sure to highlight or bold these items.

Next, go back to your 'to do' list and identify the items that you really don't want to do. Are any of these on your list because someone else asked you to do them? If so, determine why you said 'yes' to their request. Did you say 'yes' out of obligation rather than because it is an **intentional activity** towards a **goal**? If so, you have at least two choices:

Choice 1: Tell the person you changed your mind – that you do not the time or resources to be able to fulfill their request – and apologize for any inconvenience this may cause the other person. Now the item is off your 'to do' list.

Choice 2: Identify some way that this 'to do' is an **intentional activity** towards your **goal** and list it on Side #3. Highlight or bold the item.

It truly is just that simple….once you know 'The Solution' (**Chi-To-Be! Energy Surge** #10) for arriving at the decision that is most right for you! I will be teaching you 'The Solution' in Chapter 10! If you can't wait, then skip ahead to Chapter 10 and then return back to Side #3 of your Plan.

Finally, look again at your 'to do' list. All that is left are the items that you felt you needed to complete — but most likely you do not want to do them – and/or they likely do not support your **goals** or your *B-All* in any way. So, why are you doing them?

This last category of 'to do's' are the energy wasters – requiring too much effort, or too much time, or too many resources – without enough enjoyment in return to bring your energy back to balance. Completing these activities will not help you to be more 'attractive' – rather the energy spent will make you 'less attractive.' Take them off your list. Perhaps someone else you know is better suited to accomplish these tasks? If you still feel a strong obligation to complete these tasks, then skip ahead to Chapter 10 and utilize 'The Solution' to identify the real reason you have them listed on your 'to do' list and what feels best to you to do about each of the items in this category.

What Do I Do Now?

Congratulations! **Your Strategic Attraction Plan™** has been created.

I want to be clear. It's created, it's working already, yet it's not complete.

Every day, you will be encountering new people, or seeing in new ways the people you have known for years. Each day, as you encounter people you enjoy, who impress you, who inspire you, who add to your energy bank – continue to add these qualities and characteristics to Side #1.

You may be wondering what to do when you encounter people whom you don't enjoy. That's easy, too! Simply identify the qualities that are an energy drain for you. Then, determine what would be the 'flip side' of that negative quality, in other words – what would be a more positive quality than the one they demonstrated? Once you have 'flipped' the negative quality to the positive one, list the positive quality on Side #1.

Consider this addition to your Plan as a deposit into your energy bank! In this way, every experience can be an energy booster! Every day you may get a new idea, a fresh thought, or an inspiration towards how you can achieve your *B-All*. As you receive these inspirations, add these ideas to Side #3 and highlight or **bold** it.

Finally, the ultimate 'energy generation' tip about your **Strategic Attraction Plan™** is this – when you look at your Plan as soon as you awake every day for five minutes, you will start your day automatically focusing on attracting more of what you want. This practice will produce power boosts towards the fulfillment of your *B-All* to support you in achieving it with velocity and ease, just like it has for **Chi-To-Be! Master** Loralee H:

> **I've had a lot of ah-hah's.**
> *1. I've recognized habits of responding that have kept me doing the same old, same old.*
>
> *2. I've recognized perceptions that I developed during childhood that are now actually sabotaging me and holding me back.*
>
> *3. I've had ideas come for the actions to take that will get me closer to my B-All, providing much more clarity so I can be more focused and grounded in achieving on the smaller steps in addition to holding the big picture and seeing how all the parts fit together.*

My September **goals** *were:*
1. *Purchase my laptop.*
2. *Cut back hours at work, freeing up Fridays.*
3. *Follow up with my list of people to invite them to learn about Young Living® oils.*
4. *Put together my product goodie bag.*
5. *Create and order my services postcard.*
6. *Hold a successful oils class Thursday the 23rd.*

7. Have an oils party on Thursday the 16th, attracting at least 2 ideal distributors to my Young Living® community.
8. Communicate with my downline via email whenever someone places an order.
9. Support my 3 legs to reach their next respective level in the compensation plan.
10. Attract a holistic gift shop where I can share the oils with their customers on a weekly basis.

RESULTS achieved by September 30 - YAY ME!!!!!

I got my laptop today!

Sunday, I told my weekend resort job that I'm cutting back Fridays as of next week.

Attracted a new regular private client who LOVES my massage and can't live without it! That makes it easier for me to cut back Fridays at my job during the week. This will offset the income I'm giving up by cutting back hours at work.

My oils party scheduled for the 16th has to be rescheduled as the hostess isn't feeling well. However she does want to meet with me individually to learn about the oils so she is more informed when she invites people to her party when we do have it. Plus she may become another private client!

For the past couple months I've had several clients at work ask if I do private clients. I guess that's the Universe's way of telling me it's time to move into that direction.

•••••••••• RECAP ••••••••••

1 'Focusing for energy generation' means staying focused on the people who can help us to achieve our **goal(s)** faster because they either share our same **goal(s)** or they can support us in some other way.

2 Tapping into the power of the Law of Attraction will bring these people to you.

3 The **Strategic Attraction Planning Process™** featured in 'Attracting Perfect Customers…The Power of Strategic Synchronicity' by Stacey Hall and Jan Brogniez provides a formula for tapping into the power of the Law of Attraction.

4 Creating your **Strategic Attraction Plan™** is an **intentional activity** that will support all of your **goals**!

5 Continuing to add items to your Plan every day will support you in achieving your **goals** with greater velocity and ease.

6 To view a sample **Strategic Attraction Plan™**, please turn to the Appendix.

(1) Attracting Perfect Customers, The Power of Strategic Synchronicity by Stacey Hall and Jan Brogniez, copyright © by Stacey Hall and Jan Brogniez, Published by Berrett-Koehler Publishers, Inc.

chapter 5
Harmoniously Powerful Agreements

5TH CHI-TO-BE! ENERGY SURGE™

> **The Four Agreements®***
>   In the book, **The Four Agreements®**, don Miguel
> Ruiz "reveals the source of self-limiting beliefs that
> rob us of joy and create needless suffering. Based
> on ancient Toltec wisdom, **The Four
> Agreements®** offer a powerful code of conduct
> that can rapidly transform our lives to a new
> experience of freedom, true happiness, and love."
>   *(1) The Four Agreements® by don Miguel Ruiz*

I was so empowered by reading **The Four Agreements®** by don
Miguel Ruiz, I chose to consciously practice each of the
Agreements in every conversation – written and/or verbal – I
have with others in order to create more harmonious
relationships. In doing so, I have a stronger and more loving
relationship with myself.

Over 10+ years of practicing **The Four Agreements®**, I have
found each one to provide a powerful energy boost to each
intentional activity I implement on my way to fulfilling my
B-All with velocity and ease. I have also found that I am much
more powerful when I practice them in conjunction with each
other.

When we can speak in ways that attract people to us, or we can create and complete agreements in ways that leave people feeling uplifted, life is much easier, much more attractive and we are moved towards our *B-Alls* faster.

This is why I encourage each of my coaching clients to read this life-changing book and to practice these Agreements with me in our sessions.

Following is my personal interpretation and practice of each of **The Four Agreements**®. I invite you to read this powerful book to develop your own relationships with each one.

Agreement #1: Be Impeccable with Your Word™

My practice of this Agreement is to always tell the truth unless doing so would be hurtful to others. For me, it also means avoiding gossip or slander. And I feel it guides me to say what I mean with a positive intention rather than for some ill-intended purpose. And it also means, avoiding speaking about myself in a self-deprecating manner, such as "I'm not very smart about these things" or "I don't do it as well as you do" or any statement that diminishes rather than honors my greatness.

When I am being impeccable, I could say instead: "I would like to learn more about these things" or "I was not taught about these things and I would like you to share with me what you know from your experience."

I feel another aspect of impeccability is the importance of speaking only for and about 'me'. In other words, expressing my own experiences through the use of the word "I", such as "I feel," "I prefer," "I think," "I went to the store and purchased...," "I enjoyed that movie because...", etc.

This is in contrast to speaking about or including others in general statements, such as "You know when such-and-such happens you feel happy" instead of "When such-and-such happens, I feel happy."

Often when I introduce the concept of impeccability to my clients, I receive resistance to this concept because it appears to go against the guidance my clients received as children. Clients from around the world have told me they were taught the principle that it is 'wrong' to speak about ourselves. I understand that they were told it is 'egotistical' to talk about ourselves. Instead, it is better to be humble and modest.

I feel that is essential for me to acknowledge and express my own feelings, thoughts, desires, and experiences to maintain my energy at a high vibration and to attract the type of people I intend to attract to assist me in achieving my *B-All*.

On Side #1 of my **Strategic Attraction Plan™**, I list many qualities of the type of people I intend to attract to assist me. Some of these qualities are: confident, balanced, honest, caring, and compassionate. I state on Side #3 that I want people to expect me to demonstrate those same qualities. Yet, consider if I go out in the world and I start speaking statements such as, "Oh, I'm just not as smart as Nancy," or "I'm such an idiot about social networking."

● ● ● ● ● ● ● ● ● $\begin{bmatrix} \textit{Am I honoring myself?} \\ \textit{Am I demonstrating confidence?} \\ \textit{Am I demonstrating caring and} \\ \textit{compassion to myself?} \end{bmatrix}$

As I use terms that are self-deprecating, I am lowering my energy and vibration level. This means that I am now only able to attract people who are also self-deprecating (Remember, like attracts like.) And, that is probably not someone who is 'confident, balanced, honest, caring and compassionate' to themself or others.

In addition, I feel that impeccability is also expressed by the use of words that enlighten, enliven, and uplift me and others. From the standpoint of energy, words can have the power to hurt simply by lowering one's energy when we choose to use less-empowering statements.

For example, if someone is told repeatedly that they are stupid, either directly or indirectly, such as by "What you did was really stupid," they may start to believe it.

I have caught myself many a time saying to myself while at my computer, "Oh I can't believe I made that stupid typo." Or, "Oh that was such a stupid mistake, why did I do that?"

If I were to continue this practice of negative self-speak, I will subconsciously begin to believe I am stupid.

On the other hand, if I repeatedly tell myself, "I can learn this," or "I can do this," or "I am so glad I caught that typo," I will raise my confidence, which raises my energy.

Further, I love that don Miguel Ruiz also writes about 'impeccability' in choosing our words for the purpose of love. Speaking with love in my heart brings me to a place of speaking with honesty, with ethics, with integrity, and with good will. From the standpoint of the Law of Attraction, I know that speaking in this way will return the same to me.

One of the ways I like to practice impeccability is by paying attention to how often I begin a sentence with "I" versus beginning a sentence with 'You."

I invite you to watch TV and listen for how many people make a statement that is similar to, "When you do da, ta, da, ta, da, ta, this is what you get" when they are actually speaking about just about their own experience.

I love listening to interviews with celebrities. Recently, I watched one interview in which the actress was asked, "How was that experience of doing a love scene with Brad Pitt for you?" The actress began her reply with, "Well, whenever you have a love scene and you've got crew all around you…"

I had to laugh because I have not experienced being in a love scene with Brad Pitt or even been in a feature movie with the crew all around me while I was acting in a love scene!

If I was in that situation, and I was speaking with impeccability, my answer would have begun with, "Well whenever I have a love scene and I've got crew all around me…".

Another way to practice impeccability is to review Side #3 of your **Strategic Attraction Plan™** and be sure that every item on Side # 3 begins with 'I', such as "I will," "I receive," "I give," "I am," "I win," etc.

The **Chi-To-Be! Masters** offer their experiences of practicing with this Agreement:

Sandra S.

"I think if I am clear about my word, I am saying what I want and need from another person. And that person can be either in agreement with me or not. In the past, if I used 'you' or I was vague about what I was talking about, it seemed as though the conversations I would be involved with became rather mundane and/or argumentative. I know now that by

saying 'you', I'm putting something on someone else which may or may not be their experience.

When I speak from 'I', the other person can hear that is how I think. They can say, "She is not assuming that I think that way. She's not dictating that I think that way. She's giving more information about her."

I find that some people will say, "You're really nitpicky about your language." I don't spend much time with those people. Other times, I find people say, "I really like talking with you because the clarity that I get from our reactions is easy." My experience is that I don't have to say as many words when I speak from 'I'."

Maria J.

*"It is always my **intention** to act with impeccable integrity in both business and personal associations. I tend to over-extend and then in some cases have not followed through on promises because of it. (This will be added to my Plan for improvement). I have forgotten to follow through because I have not written things down. I am getting busier and busier so I have to acknowledge that everything cannot be in my head. This is where Agreement #4 comes in: I acknowledge and accept that I have done my best in all situations (even in forgetting to write things down).*

Christina L.

*"I think of these four Agreements, the most difficult for me is being impeccable with my word. Not with others, but with myself. I always keep my word to other people and am good about doing what I say I am going to do. However more recently, I would have good **intentions** to myself and write*

them down, but not keep them. I'm pretty sure one of my favorite quotes is 'The road to hell is paved with good intentions'.

One of the biggest accomplishments I have had this week is keeping up with everything I wrote down and actually doing everything within my power to achieve my monthly **goals**, *dotting i's and crossing t's. It is exhausting, but I feel a necessary and learned* **activity** *that I hope will soon become second nature."*

As I mentioned earlier, another aspect of Agreement #1 is to avoid gossip.

I have determined that it is much easier for me to avoid gossip when I start a sentence from 'I'. This is because I am speaking about my own experience, rather than about something that happened to someone else.

Even if there is another person involved in the situation I am discussing, when I choose to speak from 'I', my description is about my own experience of the situation…I am not describing or speaking about the other person.

Agreement #2: Don't Take Anything Personally™

Through don Miguel Ruiz's guidance, I have learned that I am only responsible for myself. I do not cause others to do anything. Anything they may think, do or say, to or about me, is simply a reflection of the accumulation of their own previous experiences. Again, my only responsibility is to ensure that I am being impeccable with my own word. When I truly allowed myself to understand this Agreement, I began to finally release myself from being a victim to what others think and do. In other words, I was able to take back my own power to use on my own behalf.

I utilize this Agreement in developing my **Strategic Attraction Plans™**. When I am in a situation with another person and I feel that something has been said that was hurtful or inappropriate about me, this Agreement helps me to stop and reflect before simply reacting.

First, this Agreement reminds me that what ever the person is saying…it is just their experience. It does not mean that is necessarily true about me. It's only true if I decide that it is true. Taking the time to decide if I feel it is true gives me the opportunity to pause and reflect on two aspects of my Plan:

Is this a person whose qualities match Side #1 of my **Strategic Attraction Plan™?**

If I decide that what they are saying about me is true, then is that a quality that I want people to expect of me?

In regards to the first question, if the person does not match the qualities of the people I want to attract into my life to support me in achieving my *B-All*, then their opinion of me will have much less importance to me than someone who does match those qualities.

Said another way: I may not want to be the type of person that someone who does not match the qualities I want to attract wants me to be!

$$\left[\textit{In that case, it is very easy for me to not take what they say personally.} \right]$$

• • • • • • • •

On the other hand, if this person matches the qualities of someone I do want to attract, then I am more likely to move on to the 2nd question to determine if what they are saying is something I believe is true about myself.

If I feel what someone, who I want to attract, says about me is not true, then I can choose to be 'impeccable' with my word and express that I feel differently than they do. Depending upon how they respond to me, they may or may not continue to be someone I want to attract.

If I feel what someone, who I want to attract, says about me is true, then I can determine if I want to continue to demonstrate that quality or not.

For example, as a coach, I want people to expect of me that "I am a catalyst that stirs up the status quo and believes that breakthroughs look like breakdowns at the beginning."

As a coach, I have attracted people who request for me to provide coaching to them. I explain to them at the beginning of our relationships to expect me to be a *"catalyst that stirs up the status quo and believes that breakthroughs look like breakdowns at the beginning."*

I explain that I expect them to meet the agreements that we co-create together and to be pro-active if they feel that they will not be able to meet those agreements so that we can co-create new ones together as just one way I can support them in addressing the breakdowns that will occur along the way to their breakthroughs.

Yet, over the years I have experienced a few clients whom would consistently ignore and/or break their agreements and be out of communication with me rather than be pro-active in co-creating new agreements with me.

In each case, when they did finally contact me again, they blamed me for expecting too much of them – for having unrealistic expectations of what they could achieve. In other words, they did not want me to be a 'catalyst that stirs up the status quo'.

At that point, I had a choice – I could either accept their blame and lower my expectations of what they were capable of achieving or not accept their blame and continue to be the catalyst that I want to be for people who want to achieve great and large **goals** as quickly as possible.

Since these coachees did not meet the expectations I had for my perfect clients, which choice do you think I chose?

Of course! I did not accept the blame (I did not take what they were expressing personally) and I continued to be the catalyst that I am meant to be.

At that point, they had the choice to continue to hire me as their coach or end our coaching relationship. Either of their choices had nothing to do with me…it was all about what was perfect for them to do for themselves for their Highest and Best Good.

Chi-To-Be! Master Lauren K. provides her perspective on this Agreement:

Lauren K.

"I recently read some comments people posted on a (chat) forum about me and I was not affected by what they said. I used to get upset when reading the comments others would make about me if they were negative, so I just realized that this is their reality, not mine, so I should not suffer or let what they say bother me because of their reality."

Chi-To-Be! **Master** Michael T. reveals,

 Michael T.

> *"Agreement #2 is the one I work on the most. This can be a tricky one sometimes, so I go back to basics and remember it does not matter anyway, it is all small stuff."*

Chi-To-Be! **Master** Maria J. shares so eloquently on this topic,

 Maria J.

> *"I would have to say Agreement #2 is most difficult to implement for me. If I were not thinking about myself, I would be able to see gratefully that the problem (whatever it is) is not mine. Spiritually I would say: 'Namaste'. Making a deep connection with the other to remember that love is all there is."*

Chi-To-Be! **Master** Corey S. provides insight to his relationship with Agreement #2:

 Corey S.

> *"Before reading 'The 4 Agreements,' I would allow others to 'grind my gears'. Now I realize and understand that we all have different ways in which we view life. My interpretation of a situation may be completely different from another's and, from that understanding, I can let go of whatever negative thoughts arise because I no longer allow their lives to affect mine."*

Agreement #3: Don't Make Assumptions™

I know what Assumptions do, do you?

When I am practicing Agreement #2, it is quite easy for me to be practicing Agreement #3 at the same time. When I remember that someone's response to me is based upon their own previous experiences and perceptions, then I realize that it is important for me to ask questions to clarify their reaction in order to avoid misunderstandings.

As I shared in Chapter 2, utilizing the 1st **Chi-To-Be! Energy Surge -'Schedule for Success'** – we are more likely to achieve our intended result by declaring our intentions at the start of a conversation rather than assuming that the other person has the same intended result.

Since utilizing this Agreement, I have eliminated the energy drain of unfulfilled expectations from my life.

Does that mean that I get everything I want, whenever I want it?

No.

It does mean that I am clear at the end of every conversation that I have made my intentions known; I know the other person's intentions; I know whether or not we are both interested in moving forward and what our next step will be and by when.

Regarding Agreement #3, don Ruiz reminds us all "Find the courage to ask questions and to express what you really want. Communicate with others as clearly as you can to avoid misunderstandings, sadness, and drama."

His statement reminds me of the well-worn adage: *"When I assume, I make an 'ass' out of 'u' and 'me'!"*

Chi-To-Be! Master Loralee H. offers her authentically open expression of the importance of this Agreement:

Loralee H.

"Probably the most challenging for me is to 'Not Make Assumptions.' When that creeps in, I find that because I didn't communicate clearly enough, things are left out and get complicated or twisted around. Then I have to go back and fix them, which isn't always comfortable. And it takes up time that wouldn't have had to have been spent in that way."

Chi-To-Be! Master Corey S. admits this one is a challenge for him:

 ## Corey S.

"I tend to make a lot of assumptions – It's my less-effective way of trying to understand something or someone. The best option is to just ask and get the facts. Moving forward, I will address this and be mindful of not assuming. I am sure it will allow me to reach my **goals** *more quickly, so I will be more courageous and communicate more effectively."*

Chi-To-Be! Master Sandra S. is practicing this Agreement in a new situation,

 ## Sandra S.

"I am in the adjustment process in a new employment position. Making assumptions about what my new boss would like from me could make our relationship more difficult. To the best of my ability, I am making sure to keep communication clear and open, asking questions, and avoiding passive-aggressive behavior. In working with my co-workers, I am making sure to take time and ask for what I need to be a better employee and co-worker."

This is why creating a clear and specific **Strategic Attraction Plan™** is so important to me. Creating and updating my plan provides me with the clarity and courage I need to ask the most important question of myself...as well as anyone with whom I am considering co-creating and/or maintaining a relationship.

And, the one question that I will always ask of another person when I first meet them – and it does take courage for me to do so – is, "What is the most important thing in the world to you?"

As you know from Chapter 4, this question relates to Side #2 of the **Strategic Attraction Plan™**.

I have learned from years of experience that it is easy for me to make assumptions about others based on superficial circumstances – such as how they dress, or how much money they make, or how they well they express themselves, or the types of people they attract into their lives.

I no longer believe that 'first impressions are lasting impressions' because I have found my first impressions often to be completely wrong about the other person the longer I know them. Yet, all of those distinctions are the 'filters' through which I see that person. By interacting with someone only through those filters, I am not truly interacting with the real person...only my illusion of them.

More often than not, my assumptions were incorrect and I definitely felt like an 'ass' when my dreams and expectations were not fulfilled... and I had no one to blame except myself. Thank goodness for Agreement #4!!

The only way for me to truly interact with the other person without making assumptions is to ask them to tell me about themselves in their own words...as soon as I meet them.

And, that is why the MOST important question for me to ask is "What is the most important thing in the world to you?"

In the way that the other person answers this question, I will hear who they are at their core and whether or not what is most important to them is similar to what is most important to me.

As I continue to ask open-ended questions (such as 'what does that represent to you?' or 'why is that important to you?'), I gain more information about the person…without making assumptions or putting words in their mouth.

Once I know what is in their heart, and they know what is in mine, we can co-create a relationship – be it business or social – based on that foundation.

Together, we have also formed the foundation on which to continue to build a relationship that avoids making assumptions, supports us both in achieving our *B-All*, and is empowered by Agreement #2!

Agreement #4: Always Do Your Best™

This Agreement goes hand-in-hand with our **2nd Chi-To-Be! Energy Surge – 'Do It Your Way, Any Way You Can.'** Especially when beginning a new project or starting a new relationship, it's not practical or logical to expect that I will be able to do it 'perfectly'. All I am able to do is to do the best I can in the moment with whatever knowledge and tools are available to me at that time.

Even when I am performing a task that I have previously mastered, it is illogical to expect that I will always be able to perform the task exactly the same way, to the same level, every time. Prior to being introduced to this Agreement, I would consistently be frustrated when I was not able to sustain a consistent level of success. I could not understand why I could accomplish so much in one day and then not have the same amount of energy the next day to do it again.

I now accept I am a human – not a machine. Depending upon the amount of rest I have had, the food I have eaten, the amount of energy I have already expended, my best will change minute-to-minute, hour-by-hour, day-by-day. Agreement #4 encourages me to always do my best. Yet, it also acknowledges that my best will change from one day to the next.

Chi-To-Be! Master Loralee H. shares her approach to this Agreement:

 Loralee H.

"For the most part, I've long since given up judging myself for what I did or didn't do. On any given day I give what I am able to for that time. That varies from time to time, and the **activity** *involved. When I am saturated with massage appointments, there just really isn't a whole lot left in me to give. My energy has been drained. When I'm doing things like sharing the oils with someone or explaining/ consulting with them in some way, I have a lot more energy to give because these activities are closer to my true heart's desires and interests."*

I am encouraged by **Chi-To-Be! Master** Michael T., who states:

 Michael T.

"When I do my best, I always take myself to the next level. This is what I like the most…the next level."

The only constant about Agreement #4 is to remember that our best will change moment by moment, day by day. So, let's remember **Chi-To-Be! Energy Surge #2 – Do It Your Way, Any Way You Can!**

•••••••••• **RECAP** ••••••••••

1 Agreement #1: Be Impeccable with Your Word™

"Speak with integrity. Say only what you mean. Avoid using the word to speak against yourself or to gossip about others. Use the power of your word in the direction of truth and love."*

2 Agreement #2: Don't Take Anything Personally™

"Nothing others do is because of you. What others say and do is a projection of their own reality, their own dream. When you are immune to the opinions and actions of others, you won't be the victim of needless suffering." * Remember to first identify if the person who is speaking is someone who is a perfect fit to support you in achieving your **goals** towards your *B-All* and if you wish to accept their feedback.

3 Agreement #3: Don't Make Assumptions™

"Find the courage to ask questions and to express what you really want. Communicate with others as clearly as you can to avoid misunderstandings, sadness and drama. With just this one Agreement, you can completely transform your life." *

Utilize Chi-To-Be! Energy Surge #1 – 'Schedule For Success' to ensure that you are communicating your **intentions** and asking for the other person to state their **intentions** at the start of every conversation and/or **intentional activity**. Remember that someone's response to you is based upon their own previous experiences and perceptions.

Be sure to ask questions to clarify their reaction in order to avoid misunderstandings. Practice asking, "What is the most important thing in the world to you?", as the first question you ask everyone you meet to avoid making assumptions from first impressions.

4 *Agreement #4:* Always Do Your Best™

"Your best is going to change from moment to moment; it will be different when you are healthy as opposed to sick. Under any circumstance, simply do your best, and you will avoid self-judgment, self-abuse, and regret."*

(1) **From the book The Four Agreements® ©1997, Miguel Angel Ruiz, M.D. Reprinted with permission of Amber-Allen Publishing, Inc. P.O. Box 6657, San Rafael, CA 91903. All rights reserved."*

CHI-TO-BEI

chapter 6
The Power of Love

6TH CHI-TO-BE! ENERGY SURGE™

Throughout the ages, much has been written on the subject of love, gratitude and appreciation and its powerful connection to the Law of Attraction. A search of the internet and a visit to your bookstore will provide you access to the world's greatest teachers and their various practices for expressing appreciation to expand one's ability to attract more of what is desired.

Over the years, I have learned from many of these teachers to whom I express my appreciation and love for introducing me to the essence of this concept.

As I developed a greater capacity for expressing appreciation, I also developed my own perspective of the practice of appreciation for tapping into the power of love and giving my vibration an energy surge to obtain the highest levels of attraction. My method of tapping into this continually-generating, abundant source of loving energy is what I call my **'Loving 33 Ways System™'**.

The **'Loving 33 Ways System'** is a do-it-yourself system which begins with the practice of appreciation...appreciation of our selves and others. The practice of appreciation begins with acknowledging what we already have.

This System is a method of paying closer attention ….closer attention to the finest details of what you already have. I say it's a do-it-yourself system because you will create your own **intentional activities** of the System to fit your **goal**(s) once you understand the two major principles of the System.

Over my many years as a coach, the majority of my clients have sought my assistance because they felt that something was missing in their lives and/or their businesses. They felt that they were lacking in some skill or quality or knowledge. Or, they felt that they did not have enough customers or enough funding for a project. Or, they felt that they were missing out on life because they did not have a romantic partner.

In other words, in my experience, most people seek help from a coach or other expert because they feel they are missing something.

You may say, "But, of course! Why else would someone ask for assistance?"

My answer is this:

There are always multiple ways to address any situation and multiple perspectives from which to view any situation. I choose to make it a practice to look for the solutions and perspectives that keep my energy at a high level of attractiveness.

I suggest to my clients to address the situation – not by attempting to improve what they are lacking or filling a void – but, rather by intending to receive support to attract more of what they desire!

Remember our 1st **Chi-To-Be! Energy Surge** is 'Scheduling Your Success.' Any **activity** we plan and implement towards our **goals** is an **intentional activity**! Meeting with a coach is just one **intentional activity** towards a **goal**(s).

Yet, even before requesting support from a coach or a friend, you can practice appreciation on your own by first acknowledging what you already have.

Again, in my experience with myself and my clients, I notice how often what is already attracted is quickly taken for granted. Once acquired, it is no longer valued as highly as it was when it was still in the process of being attracted.

Principle #1 of the **'Loving 33 Ways System,'** is to view what you have already acquired as even more valuable than those items which you are still in the process of attracting. *The Appreciation Perspective Experience* is the process for doing just that. By scheduling and completing the following *Appreciation Perspective Experience* as an **intentional activity** towards your **goal**(s), you will first identify and then appreciate the full value of what you already have that is already pointing or moving you in the direction towards your **goal**(s) …a very empowering exercise!

I have found that the simple practice of acknowledging and appreciating what I already have often brings me more of what I desire simply, easily and with velocity.

I will also admit that the challenge for me is to stay focused on what I already have – to admire it from every angle – without focusing on what I have not yet attracted. Said another way – sometimes it is hard to stay focused on what I have rather than what I don't have yet!

That's why I call this a 'practice'. Utilizing our **2nd Chi-To-Be! Energy Surge** is **'Do It Your Way, Any Way You Can'** will help.

I do my best to stay focused on the intended result for this practice, which is to express as much appreciation as possible for what I have already attracted to me.

As thoughts come to me of what more I desire (notice I said 'what more I desire' instead of 'what I am lacking'), I list those desires on Side #1 and/or Side #3 of my **Strategic Attraction Plan™**. This is how to apply our 4th **Chi-To-Be! Energy Surge – Focusing For Energy Generation** – for even greater support. By listing them on the Plan, I am no longer worried or concerned about what I have not yet attracted. I know I will be attracting it in the perfect time and the perfect way.

Empowered by this certainty, I am now able to stay focused for greater amounts of time on expressing appreciation for what I already have attracted...and so will you!

Appreciation Perspective Experience

Before continuing with this Chapter, please schedule 10 minutes to focus on one of your **goals** and what you have already attracted into your life that is pointing or moving you towards that **goal**. I encourage you to schedule this **activity** on your calendar as an **intentional activity** towards your **goal**.

If your **goal** is to attract more customers, focus on the customers you already have. If you do not have any customers yet, then what aspects of your life and/or business can you acknowledge as indicators that are pointing or moving you in the direction of your **goal** to have attracted customers?

Perhaps you just received your first order of printed business cards – you can acknowledge the business cards as the indicators of the customers who will be doing business with you as a result of receiving your card. Perhaps you are a customer of another person's business. Acknowledge and appreciate all the ways that you are a great customer of that business as an indicator of the qualities your own future customers will demonstrate to you. As you identify your great qualities, remember these qualities are wonderful items to use to describe the customers you want to attract. So, be sure to list them on Side #1 of your **Strategic Attraction Plan™**, too. You may wish to acknowledge and appreciate each time you expand your list.

Let's take another **goal** – you may intend to write and publish a book.

First, I encourage you to acknowledge yourself as an 'author.' Early in my writing career, I received this splendid tip. I was asked what I do and I replied, "I am in the process of writing a book."

The person said, *"Oh, you are an author."*

And, I said, *"No. The book isn't published yet."* To which the person replied, *"If you are already in the process of writing…even if it's just your journal…you are an author."*

From that moment forth, I acknowledged myself as an author. And, when I introduced myself as an author to others, it was amazing to me how quickly I received recommendations and connections to other authors, agents and publishers – who I know I would not have been attracted to me any other way!

Back to you and your **goal** of writing a book – if you have an idea for your book, be sure to acknowledge the idea and spend time focusing on the idea and look at it from all the angles and perspectives – as if you are looking at it through a magnifying glass. The more focus given to the idea, the faster the book will take shape and manifest. Perhaps you have recently purchased a desk at which to write – or you already had the desk – either way, practice acknowledging the desk because you have a structure sturdy enough on which to write your best-seller. If you have already had a book published and you are planning on writing others, focus on all the wonderful experiences you have had as a published author. As you receive thoughts of what more you would like to experience with your future books, list those ideas on Side 3 your **Strategic Attraction Plan™**.

Let's take one more **goal** – perhaps you have a **goal** to be married and you are not yet in a committed relationship with another person.

Having been in that situation myself, I can offer this suggestion towards the practice of appreciation: acknowledge and appreciate yourself as much as possible!

What I learned from my own experience is that what does not work is to focus on the 'lack' of a romantic partner and/or the 'wanting' of the romantic partner. All I was able to attract from the age of 17 until 34, with my focus on lack and wanting, was more lack and wanting.

At the age of 34, I received a tip to stop focusing on what was missing in my life and I changed my perspective to start focusing on what was already great about me. By appreciating myself, I began sending out energy signals that I honor and value myself – that I am loveable. This is when I began the practice of acknowledging myself. After just a few weeks of consciously acknowledging myself, I created my first – and very rough – version of an attraction plan – actually more of a list of what I wanted to attract, as well as I what I had to offer to the relationship. Two days after creating this plan, I was introduced to the man who is now my husband. We were engaged within 3 weeks and we were married within 4 months! And, yes, we are still happily married 19 years later.

So, I believe with all my heart that it works to acknowledge all the qualities that make you loveable and ready for marriage.

Acknowledge all the ways that you treat yourself well.

Acknowledge all the tangible and energetic gifts you give to yourself and others that will be the same gifts that you will give to your spouse. Acknowledge all the ways that you give yourself experiences of what is most important to you (this is the answer you wrote on Side #2 of your **Strategic Attraction Plan™**).

These are all aspects of what you already have/own towards being in the type of marriage you desire! And, these are the qualities that will attract to you the mate who is a perfect match for those qualities through the Law of Attraction. And, of course, as you focus and magnify these qualities, you will identify many more items to add to Side #1 and Side #3 of your **Strategic Attraction Plan™**, which will attract the fulfillment of this **goal** with velocity and ease.

I encourage you to implement the *Appreciation Perspective Experience (A.P.E.)* at least once every day as you will be attracting new people, blessings and gifts throughout each day to acknowledge and appreciate. In other words – forgive the pun – encourage yourself to go *A.P.E.* with joy and appreciation every day to tap into the power of love.

Chi-To-Be! **Master** Maria J. goes *A.P.E.* every morning.

 Maria J.

> *"My morning begins with gratitude for the roof over my head and running water. I spend a few minutes picturing life without what I consider 'basics'; which many in the world may not have. Without these basics my* **goals** *could not be imagined. I would be in survival mode. This focus allows me to appreciate how really wealthy I am. Wanting more then becomes not merely a* **goal***, but an obligation to serve."*

Showing The Love For What You've Got

After implementing your *A.P.E.*s, you are now ready to adopt the 2nd Principle of the **'Loving 33 Ways System'** – *Showing The Love For What You've Got!*

Again, consider your **goal(s)**. To achieve your **goal(s)**, do you intend to attract more clients and/or customers? Do you intend to attract more purchasers of your books? Do you intend to attract a business investor? Do you intend to attract more friends? Do you intend to attract more and better employees? Do you intend to attract your life partner?

During your *A.P.E.* experiences, you are identifying what you already have and mentally focusing on the gratitude and appreciation you have for what you already have attracted.

Utilizing this 2nd Principle of the **'Loving 33 Ways System,'** you will be implementing more tangible **activities** to express appreciation for what you have already attracted.

For example, if you intend to attract more customers and you already have at least one customer, you will be implementing tangible **activities** to love 33 ways on that one customer until more customers start coming your way.

If you intend to write a book and you have attracted an idea for the book, then you will be implementing tangible **activities** to love 33 ways on that idea until it manifests into a best-seller.

If you intend to attract a life partner and you are not currently dating someone – yet, you do have friends – you will be implementing tangible **activities** to love 33 ways on you and your friends until that love attracts your life partner to you.

Returning for just a moment back to the concept of 'taking for granted' what is already attracted, consider this: How many times have you seen companies offer marketing programs that are only available to new customers, such as discounted cell phone plans made available only to customers the company does not have yet? The cell phone industry is one of the most hotly competitive industries. In my personal opinion, I believe it is exactly for this reason – the most loyal customers are not appreciated/valued as much as customers of competitive companies. My personal belief is that if any company offered its best service and discount plans according to the length of time a customer has stayed with the company, with its longest term customers receiving the best deals, it would encourage more loyalty and more word-of-mouth praise from these loyal customers. Word-of-mouth praise has been proven to be much more credible than mass media advertising and often results in more new customers. It's also much less expensive than mass media advertising.

Bottom line: the energy of competitive discounts is draining and the energy of appreciation is empowering.

During a coaching session with a client, I introduced the '**Loving 33 Ways System**' and I asked my client to think about a business that she supports. She mentioned a restaurant in her neighborhood.

I asked, *"How many times during the last year would you say that the restaurant owners or managers pro-actively let you know how much they appreciate you."*

She said: *"Quite often, about six times. That's why I continue to go."*

I asked: *"How do they let you know they appreciate you?"*

She answered: *"If I order an entrée, they bring me a cup of soup without charging me. They bring me tea at no charge. I held a party there, and they gave me a gift."*

I asked: *"If you have not been to the restaurant for a while, do they contact you or do anything to get you to come in?"*

She said: *"Actually, no."*

I then inquired: *"How many people have you introduced to that business?*

She answered: *"I brought close to 30 people to the restaurant for the party."*

I asked one more question: *"If the restaurant contacted you in-between your visits, would it change how often you visit the restaurant?*

She said: *"I might go more often. If they reminded me, I probably would show up more often."*

Now, back to you – if you are in the process of attracting more clients/customers, consider if you would like someone to bring 30 customers right to you just that quick. Or, if you are intending to attract book buyers, how would you like for each person who purchases your book to also attract 30 more people to instantly buy your book?

It's very possible if you choose to implement the **'Loving 33 Ways System.'**

Even though the restaurant my client frequented did nothing to get her in the door, they made sure that she keeps coming back by taking special care of her when she is in the restaurant to let her know she is appreciated. The free cup of soup and tea, the gift given at the party, these are all tangible displays of affection – and are what keep my client returning to the restaurant and bringing her friends with her.

Further, she stated she would frequent the restaurant even more often if they had a system for staying in contact with her in-between visits.

If they had their own version of the **'Loving 33 Ways System,'** the restaurant's owners would most likely see many more of their most loyal customers more often.

Consider your favorite restaurant or clothing store or hair salon or massage therapist. Do you agree that you use their services because they make you feel appreciated when they are serving you? Would you use their services more, or recommend them to others more, if they kept in touch with you in-between visits?

My favorite restaurant is Fleming's Prime Steakhouse & Wine Bar http://www.flemingssteakhouse.com/. Even though it is a 'chain' restaurant with locations around the country, I feel like my local Fleming's is privately owned. Yes, it is considered to be a fine dining restaurant. So, I would expect good service.

However, the attention I receive at Fleming's is far superior to any other fine dining restaurant I have experienced. Jackie Evon, the Operating Partner, made a point to get to know my husband and me by name; when I gave a compliment to a server, it was noted in my personal guest record and that person is my designated server every time I visit the restaurant; my food allergies are also noted in my guest record along with what I have ordered in the past and, if I call ahead, Chef Travis will create special appetizer and entrée choices for me that are not on the menu. More importantly, I receive announcements from the restaurant every month about special events, seasonal menu selections, as well as recipes I can prepare at home. They also often have special pricing on certain menu items for their loyal guests.

Do I feel loved? Absolutely!!

● ● ● ● ● ● ● ● *Does this type of appreciation happen by accident – Absolutely Not!*

Fleming's **B-All** for its customers is stated as: Our goal is to provide an ongoing celebration of exceptional food and wine, in the company of friends and family. We think you'll find the atmosphere inviting, the spirit generous and joyful, and the overall experience one you won't soon forget.

The company's **goals** towards this **B-All** , which each Fleming's associate has adopted, are stated as 'Fleming's Principles and Beliefs':

———●●——●———

For our associates, the soul of Fleming's is rooted in our Principles and Beliefs. These originate from our founders' love of people, our passion for the restaurant business and our belief that people are inherently good and seek a sense of belonging and significance. Our spirit comes to life by living these Principles and Beliefs every day in all our restaurants:

Trust — we keep our promises. Our word and our follow-through are the most precious things we own. It is the foundation of our integrity and it makes everything else possible.

Fun — we always work to keep the Fleming's experience fresh for all Our People. It is having a sense of humor about yourself, sharing your zest for life and celebrating the success of others every chance we get.

Excellence — we show our passion for results every day. It is embracing our standards, executing perfectly, attending to the details of every detail, giving the best of yourself, and welcoming the challenge to improve and grow.

Balance — we expect to live a full, rich life. We understand and respect the connection between "work" and "play."

Respect — we put the dignity of people first. It is being courteous, listening without interrupting, showing high regard for differences in perspective, and honoring the individuality of Our People.

Hospitality — we see to the well-being and comfort of Our People. It is being warmly welcoming, kind, generous, inclusive of all people, and caring in attitude and action.

The **intentional activities** towards these **goals** are all the ways that I stated above that I feel loved when I am in the restaurant and in-between my visits:

Intentional Activity #1:

The manager made a point to get to know my husband and me by name

Intentional Activity #2:

When I gave a compliment to a server, it was noted in my personal guest record and that person is my designated server every time I visit the restaurant.

Intentional Activity #3:

My food allergies are also noted in my guest record along with what I have ordered in the past.

Intentional Activity #4:

When I call ahead, the chef will plan ahead certain special appetizer and entrée choices, not on the menu, just for me and my husband.

Intentional Activity #5:

I receive e-mail announcements from the restaurant every month about special events, seasonal menu selections, as well as recipes I can prepare at home.

Intentional Activity #6:

> They also often have special pricing on certain menu items for their loyal guests and I am notified of these specials via e-mail (my preferred method).

This is Fleming's own system of loving its guests. Let us now proceed with how you can create your own System.

33 Times A Year

Various consumer behavior studies have shown that it takes an average of 33 different contacts with a customer for them to feel appreciated by the business. That's 33 proactive contacts after the person has become a customer! The term 'proactive' means the company or business makes the first move rather than waiting for a customer to make a request.

I am sure you will agree with me that most companies, especially small businesses, don't initiate even one proactive activity. So, it is completely understandable why most business owners would say they want/need more customers and why they are not receiving as many referrals from their current customer base as they would like.

Let's discuss now a few of the 33 ways to love what you have already attracted.

At this point, it is important to have your **Strategic Attraction Plan™** in front of you and turned to Side #3 so that you can list each of your 33 **intentional activities** for **Loving 33 Ways** on the person or group of people you are intending to attract towards the fulfillment of your *B-All*.

I'm going to start you off with a few ideas of ways that you can proactively show the love. Not all of these ideas will fit every type of relationship. Choosing what is appropriate for the person or group of people you want to attract is part of the 'do-it-yourself' aspect of this System.

1. **Advance notice of contacts:** Always be sure the first of your 33 contacts is to let your perfect people know that you will be in regular communication because building a relationship with them is important to you. In the Introduction to this book, I mentioned that I am a Certified Aromatherapy Coach and I am also a representative for an essential oils company. When I assist someone to open their own essential oils distributor account, I let them know that I am going to be sending them a lot of information about essential oils to support them in knowing how to use the oils most effectively. I also explain that the first email I will be sending is information about four different websites where they can access information on their own, so that they're not dependent on me. I explain that I will be calling and sending emails to invite them to the various events and gatherings I host and facilitate. If they tell me they prefer for me to not contact them, then I know immediately they will not be my most perfect distributor team members. Why? Because I have listed on Side #1 of my Plan that my perfect team members desire to receive the information and feel honored that I love them in 33 different ways each year!

2. **Birthday cards** – as you attract the person or group of people you desire, make a point to ask each person to provide you with their birth date. Then, send an email or snail mail card to arrive on that date to let them know you honor the day they were born.

3. Educational information – Most of the time, when we think about sharing educational information, we think of sharing information about us and our company or our ideas. However, a more effective way of showing the love as you attract the person or group of people you intend to attract is to determine their personal and professional interests so that you can periodically send them information that is specifically relevant to those interests. For example, one of your perfect clients may be planning a vacation to an exotic locale. You can help save them time and show your love by researching interesting websites about that locale and forwarding the list of the sites to your client…or even purchase a tourist guide to the location and present it to your client.

4. Calling just to say 'hello' – In this age of rampant texting and email messages, an actual phone call has become a special way to show the love. I often pick up the phone just to check in and say hi to people who are most perfect in supporting me in fulfilling my *B-All* Why? Because this is the most effective way to actually build a friendship with these people. For me a true friendship involves being just as concerned about their lives as I want them to be about mine. That can't happen through email and texting alone. I keep a list of all my 'perfect people' that I look at daily. The list has hundreds of names on it. At least once a month – and usually much more often – I will pick up the phone to call one or more of the people on my list to see how they are doing. To be clear, these phone calls are in addition to any other communication I may have with them regarding our mutual projects. These are not 'sales' calls. These are 'building a friendship' calls that I make to all of my clients (friends)…just because!

One of my clients shared that she realized that building a friendship through 'hello' calls is working for her investment counselor. He calls her every month just to 'check in' and see how she is doing. He does not discuss her investments during these 'check in' calls. Yet, she finds herself dropping into his office each month with more money to deposit into her account for him to invest because she knows he is sincerely interested in her best interests. They have developed a friendship.

Chi-To-Be! Master Christina L. shares,

Christina L.

"I love, for no reason at all, doing little acts of kindness or unexpected texts or phone calls to people telling them how much I appreciate them. I notice their accomplishments and tell them how proud I am of them.

5. Referrals – If you wish to receive referrals, then consider being someone who attracts opportunities to provide referrals. For example, if you have attracted an investor or a sponsor, consider loving that investor or sponsor by intending to attract other opportunities that you can refer to them. If you have attracted a literary agent, be on the look-out for other authors this agent may be interested in representing. If you have attracted a distributor/salesperson to represent your products, assist that person by directing referrals their way ... especially at the beginning when they are just in the **Seeding** stage of attracting their own clients on your behalf. I make this a regular practice for new essential oil distributors I attract, who also want to be 'business builders.' This is one of my **goals** and it is in the *BLOOMING* stage because, when I open a wholesale account for these new essential oil users, I will open it under one of my 'business builder' distributors. In doing so, we both receive a commission from the same order. I also connect the 'business builder' with the new distributor as a way of giving added support to the new distributor...as they say 'two heads are better than one.' In this way, we all win! During the writing of this book, I was contacted by someone who wanted my support in promoting their workshop in the New York area. I live on the West Coast so I wasn't a perfect fit for project. Instead, I referred that person to **Chi-To-Be! Master** Sandra S. She has done similar projects on the East Coast before and she was able to provide the person with exactly the support they needed.

6. 'Something Extra' – At one time, frequent customer discount cards were special. However, they have been used so extensively in every type of business that there is now an expectation that a company offers such a bonus for a certain number of visits or amount of purchase. In addition to a frequent customer card, offer 'Something Extra' to those people who you truly want to love. Something extra can be an unexpected cup of soup with an entrée (as mentioned previously) or a gift given for no particular reason. The first time a client books a **Raindrop Technique** appointment with me, they receive a frequent loyalty card (book 10 appointments, receive 1 free) and also a 'something extra,' which is always an unexpected gift – perhaps an essential oil sample, sometimes oil-infused bath salts, etc. Since the first appointment will determine whether another appointment will be booked, I want my clients to know immediately that I will always provide more than they expect. To the participants in the **Chi-To-Be! Mastery Program**, I often provide bonus tips at no-charge.

Chi-To-Be! Master Lauren K. has these ideas for 'something extra,'

Lauren K.

"I give random, thoughtful gifts. They don't have to be expensive, just something small that reminds me of that person like a card or a candy bar that has a funny name. It's the thought that counts."

Chi-To-Be! Master Maria J. gives 'something extra' in this way:

Maria J.

"I always give my perfect people extra massage session time at no cost. This is because they are committed to getting well and they are committed to using my services to do so."

7. Vacation notice – One of the kindest ways to let our perfect people know we care about them is to let them know in advance when we will be unavailable and for how long. In this age of technology, it is possible to set a vacation notice on an automatic responder to their email messages, as well as to change our voice mail messages to announce when we will be out of the office or unavailable for any reason. Consider this – have you ever left a voice mail message or sent an email message and wondered why the person wasn't responding - only to find out later that they were out of town or out of the country? If you found that to be frustrating, you are not alone. One of the easiest and kindest ways to let people know that they are important is to communicate with them…and especially to be proactive in advance of periods of time when you will not be able to communicate with them. Even if you're not out of town – let's say you just want to take a day away from the office and you're not going to respond to a phone call or email – go ahead and put a message on your email. Change the message on your phone; here's a suggestion: "I'll be away from email today. I'm not returning phone calls until such and such day".

8. 'Did You Know Time is Almost Up' calls – One of my clients sells home appliance warranties. She makes a point to call her customers long before the warranty is due to expire because she knows that they probably are not aware of the expiration date. Her intention for calling is not to sell them another warranty. Her intention is to encourage them to have an

THE POWER OF LOVE

inspection of their appliances scheduled well before the warranty expires so any appliance can be fixed under the current warranty, if necessary. As a result, the majority of her customers renew their warranties.

I make similar contacts with my essential oil distributors to let them know when their account will be expiring due to non-**activity**. I call to be sure they know, if they place another order before the account expires, they will avoid having to purchase a 'Starter Kit' again. Also, I ensure they know the company has a program that provides points towards free products when a person places an order every month.

Then, when I notice that someone on this program misses their shipment date, I call the person immediately to ensure that they know to call the company to redeem any points accrued before the end of the month or they will lose those points. At the beginning of implementing this loving **activity** I was concerned that my customers would feel pressure from me to place another order. However, I chose to trust that they would feel the sincerity of my intention.

Here are just two of the many uplifting and empowering experiences I have had as a result of making these 'Did You Know Time is Almost Up' calls…

> **Distributor #1:**
> Her husband lost his job and she was having trouble making ends meet; I asked her when was the last time she cashed in her reward points and she told me she has never cashed in her points…she had forgotten that she was earning points. This distributor has been on the rewards program for almost 2 years…she had accrued

hundreds of points! She called the corporate office the same day to redeem the points for oils and other products she needed, but could not afford to purchase!

Distributor #2: Her family was in a car accident; her husband and daughter had serious medical conditions; she did not realize that she had not placed her rewards order that month. Also, she had forgotten that she was earning points with every order and had not cashed in her points for the entire time – almost 3 years! She called the corporate office that same day to cash in her points to get the products she needed to help her family!

Here's a few more suggestions of ways to Love, Love, Love offered by **Chi-To-Be! Master** Sandra S.:

Sandra S.

*I have my radio guests in a separate list on Twitter. When they have an upcoming event, or a new book published, I retweet or post something about them to my followers.

*I post new links and updates to my social network pages for my perfect customers. I share tools, books, etc. on my blog and social media sites that could make life easier or more fun.

*I make introductions: A person I worked with wanted an introduction to someone well-known in the Social Media world. I saw that the person they were interested in published an article in their newsletter that dovetailed nicely with my client. I went on Twitter and introduced them and they have now connected.

And, a few more offered by **Chi-To-Be! Master** Tara R.

 Tara R.

"I feel I have not spent enough time supporting and Love, Love, Loving my Young Living® team members and coaching clients with whom I have been blessed right now. One of my **goals** *is to create and implement 33 ways to love these team members and coaching clients.*

I started last week by offering to pick up one of my team members/coaching clients and bring her to a local farmers market to show her around. Not only did she appreciate this, but I felt so blessed to have this time with her, and we both learned a lot from the local farmers.

I loved another client in this way: instead of simply dropping off prepared chicken broth as I usually do, I brought the supplies over and we made a batch together. I received the blessing of supporting my client in creating responsibility and ownership of her own health recovery. An unexpected, and equally great, by-product is her husband LOVED coming home to the smell of the broth cooking and is now making his own health changes.

From these experiences, I have grown to realize that I am now able to honestly appreciate and perceive with gratitude any illnesses or issues that I or my family or friends are experiencing. I believe these ailments give me a 'heads up' to pay attention; a gift of a loud and clear message, 'Something is out o balance. Please tend to it.' I have found over and over when the message is heeded and measures are taken to heal, there is a great blessing to be gained from the experience."

Whatever activities you intend to implement in your **'Loving 33 Ways System™,'** be sincere in loving the people in your life. The natural reaction you will receive in return is the same amount of sincerity and love. It is how the Law of Attraction works.

Conversely, if any activities are implemented as a manipulation, that energy will be felt and love is not what you will receive in return. Said another way: garbage in, garbage out, right?

Put love in, love comes back; especially from the people with whom it is most perfect to be in relationship.

Another aspect of sincerity is taking responsibility for our actions and/or our non-actions. One of my clients let me know that if he has been out of communication with his customers for more than a couple of months, he calls to apologize for not staying in touch. I expect that most of his customers would be wonderfully surprised by this gesture. Even though they were not expecting to hear from him at all, he knew that he was not implementing all the **intentional activities** as planned towards his **goal**. And, he wants his customers to expect him to do what he says he will do. By calling and apologizing for the delay in making contact, his customers can have a greater degree of trust that he values them as people…not just customers.

Chi-To-Be! Master Olivia B. shares that she is implementing a similar loving **activity** – for all the people in her life:

 Olivia B.

> *"I am calling the people/friends/colleagues I have not contacted in months by getting rid of the excuse that 'they are just fine' and committing to my intention to show them more love and appreciation. I am listening to that part of me that wants to give a sweet friendly gesture and silencing that part of*

me that creates an excuse to do something else instead. I am conforming less to what my conditioning has cornered me into, and expressing more creativity and self love...this one is for me so that it transmutes to others."

Before moving on to the next Chapter, I encourage you to stop here and add to Side #3 of your Plan all the **intentional activities** you expect yourself to implement each year as part of your own **'Loving 33 Ways System".**

Chi-To-Be! Master Valerie M. is adjusting her schedule to make room for her 33 connections a year:

Valerie M.

"I am scheduling time on Friday for my 'just because' correspondence. I find that if I schedule and write it down, I will do it without having to think about it. This is particularly useful for me because it doesn't give me a chance to think my way out of it."

•••••••••• **RECAP** ••••••••••

1 Tapping into the power of love is one of the fastest ways to give your vibration an energy surge to obtain the highest levels of attraction.

2 The **'Loving 33 Ways System'** is a do-it-yourself system which begins with the practice of appreciation...appreciation for one's self and others. The practice of appreciation begins with acknowledging what we already have attracted.

3 Principle #1 of the **'Loving 33 Ways System,'** is to first value what you already have attracted even more than what you still want to acquire using the *Appreciation Perspective Experience.*

4 The intended result for this practice is to express as much appreciation as possible for what has already been attracted.

5 Encourage yourself to go *A.P.E.* with joy and appreciation every day to tap into the power of love

6 The 2nd Principle of the **'Loving 33 Ways System'** is **Showing The Love For What You've Got** by implementing more tangible **intentional activities** to express gratitude and appreciation for what has already been attracted.

7 Before moving on to the next Chapter, list on Side #3 of your Plan each of your 33 tangible **intentional activities** for loving the person or group of people you are intending to attract towards the fulfillment of one of your **goals** towards your *B-All*. For example, one of your 33 **activities** you could add to Side 3 might be "I send an e-mail birthday card to each one of the people who match this Plan." Consider what other **intentional activities** you can implement as part your own **"Loving 33 Ways System."**

chapter 7
Chi Generating Rituals

A common definition of 'to generate' is 'to bring into being.'(1) By this definition, then a **Chi-Generating Ritual** can be any **intentional activity** to be implemented to bring a **goal**, or ultimately a *B-All*, closer to fulfillment…or 'into being.

More importantly, a **Chi-Generating Ritual** is intended to be the activating and catalyzing force behind every other **intentional activity** undertaken each day.

• • • • • • •
> *"Rituals are actions performed regularly with conscious and unconscious expectations. All rituals focus and activate our inner power. Ritual characteristics include cycles of repetitive actions performed in a specific way that do not have strong functional or logical content, but do have strong personal meaning." (2)*

Chi-To-Be! Master Olivia B. has been creating rituals for a number of years. She offers these insights for your consideration:

Olivia B.

> *"I feel that ritual can be many actions. Every ancient and modern culture has ritual. Our children pledge allegiance to the flag; that is ritual. If we join in Matrimony, there are specific words spoken to complete the ritual. Natives of the Americas have many rituals that have created a feeling of mysticism and earthiness around such peoples. In my experience, most people have ritual or routine- agreements we have with ourselves that say, 'this is something I will do regularly because it serves me or the group I am serving.'*
>
> *A wise woman once said 'don't even think about praying until you are 'checked in' for prayer'. I loved her enthusiasm when making this statement, she was a fierce praying woman who was basically saying, if you are not in alignment, your prayers don't go very far, and this is a message that many masters hum at different rhythms.*
>
> *What is alignment? My understanding of alignment is a sense of knowing or deep core consciousness. It is the reason Yoga is practiced, so that our body temples can sit in alignment for longer periods of time free of blocks and barriers, allowing the light of the soul star to flood into every vein, corner and cell of the body."*

A **Chi-Generating Ritual** is performed every day…either at the beginning or the end or at both the beginning and the end of the day.

You may already have a Chi-Generating Ritual that you do every day, just like **Chi-To-Be!**T **Master** DeZ O.:

Dez O.

"My morning and evening ritual is something that is as much a part of me as breathing. It begins before I am fully conscious – in the 'awake, not awake' cycle of waking up in the morning. While I don't have a set routine, there is a basic foundation I have to build upon according to how I am feeling at the present moment. I think of it as "co-creating" my day with the Universe.

I just start telling the Universe what I want my day to be like. I connect with my Higher Self, my God-self, my 'I AM' self. Next, I connect and have a conversation with one of my Angels, Ascended Masters, or a Guide of Higher Intelligence. I start the conversation by saying 'Today is going to be an awesome day and all the right people, situations, resources will be there at the right time when I need it exactly in a way that only the results in my highest good of pure Divine Bliss!' I enjoy being amazed and surprised how the Universe brings it all together for me.

Next I make morning tea, adding Young Living® 'Frankincense' and 'Thieves' oils. I then burn Frankincense resin and do my distant healings scheduled for the day, followed by my meditations, my angel oracle reading or I read from great spiritual teachings. Some days I do all, some days I do one or two of these things. Some days I am guided to none of the above in the morning and guided to do something else. Eventually sometime throughout the day I am guided to take time to do one or two of them. I follow my intuition and go with the flow of what in the moment.

Throughout the day, I have a quick appreciation conversation with my "Divine Personal Managers.' This amplifies my focus of 'keep it simple and enjoy the present moment.' If an

activity *does not feel good, I know that is a sign to ask myself 'why am I doing this'? In that moment I can choose to either keep feeling miserable doing what I am doing or choose to get back in the flow of feeling good.*

At night, before I snuggle in my bed to go to sleep, I send appreciation for my day to the Universe and send prayers for my friends, family, and Mother Earth. I ask to keep me safe should this be a night that I travel (astral-travel) to heal others on a Soul Level. I ask to remember any teachings that I may receive from the Ascended Masters. I ask that I may sleep peacefully and awake healthy and happy to begin a new day full of passion and exciting adventures!

All I know is this works for me. I have an incredible amazing life. This passion I have for life did not come over night. Ten years ago I would have just given up and lived in sadness, anger, & misery. That is not even an option today and never will be again. I learn every day just how much power I have in creating the world of my choice. No one can do that for me nor take that away from me. This is how my daily rituals empower me...to love my life!"

Rituals Can Be Simple

Do you have to create a ritual as elaborate as the one shared by DeZ? Absolutely not. A **Chi-Generating Ritual** is any **intentional activity** that you wish to create as your activating and catalyzing force for all of your other **intentional activities**.

Does it have to involve prayer? Absolutely not.

Perhaps spending time with your family in the morning and/or in the evening is what generates and amplifies your energy. Perhaps it is taking your dog for a walk or taking a morning swim.

The length of time of the **activity** and the type of **activity** is not important…what is important is that you have a **Chi-Generating Ritual** of your own.

Turning Your Plan Into A Daily Ritual

Earlier in this book, I stated that it is important to look at our **Strategic Attraction Plans™** every day to remain focused on your *B-All*. This **intentional activity** is an activating and catalyzing force behind every other **intentional activity** – which is why I consider creating a Plan to be a **Chi-Generating Ritual**.

By reviewing and adding items to your Plan before going to bed, you are creating your **Chi-Generating Ritual** of preparing yourself to wake up and start your day in a way that ensures you will move closer to your **goals**. By taking the time to create a nightly ritual of meditating on Side #3 of your **Strategic Attraction Plan™**, you can envision how you want your next day to be…what you would like to be improving the next day…what types of people and opportunities you intend to attract the next day…and the outcome you intend to achieve as a result of every **intentional activity** planned for the next day. As you sleep, your sub-conscious mind can prepare the way for you. And, when you awaken, you will be prepared to start the day that you already created.

Of course, you can also create this as a morning wake-up ritual to prepare for your day's success. Before leaving the comfort of your bed, give yourself a moment to meditate on what is the most important thing in the world to you (written on Side #2 of your Plan) as well as envisioning each of your **intentional activities** for the day being fulfilled.

I find it is easier for me to create this **Chi-Generating Ritual** at the end of my day when I can still remember the day's experiences.

Recapitulation and Casting

A **Chi-Generating Ritual** that I incorporate along with meditating on my *B-All* and my daily **intentional activities** is called 'Recapitulation and Casting'. I was first introduced to this practice of 'Recapitulation and Casting' in February 2002 during my Nia Technique® White Belt Teacher Training (www.NiaNow.com).

Done at the end of the day, as stated in the Nia Technique® White Belt Manual (March 2001), the practice of Recapitulation involves sitting
> *"quietly, with the body relaxed and your mind and emotions in a neutral state. Allow yourself to reflect on a past experience by checking into the body and sensing what it remembers, noticing its temperature or patterns of release or tension. Relive the experience by sensing it in your body rather than thinking about it."*

Casting, according to the Nia Technique® White Belt Manual (March 2001), is the process of skimming
> *"over the main ideas for the following day. Notice if you make automatic assumptions about the topic to come. Notice if you think you already know what it is, and then close down to the option of new learning and presence. Notice if you open wide to the possibility, and most importantly notice how your body responds to it all. Casting is a way of warming up the body, not the mind, and introducing it to the themes to come. Do not assume. Be impeccable with the truth — you have never experienced what will happen tomorrow. Experiment and enjoy."*

As I prepare to sleep each night, I relive my **activities** over the course of the day, I feel the experiences of when I did and did not speak my truth. I feel when I did and did not make assumptions. I feel when I did and did not take things personally. And, I feel when I did and did not do my best.

In the early days of practicing Recapitulation, it was difficult for me to stop dwelling on parts of my day that did not go as well as I would have liked. When I remembered to also utilize 'The 4 Agreements™' – especially remembering that I did the best I could that day, it made it easier to accept that the day was done, to learn what I had to learn from each experience, and then move on to Casting.

• • • • • • • •
> *It became even easier when I began to celebrate my day by going A.P.E. (my Appreciation Perspective Experience) immediately after Recapitulating and before Casting.*

Once I have re-lived the day and acknowledged and expressed appreciation for everything I attracted during that day, I then cast forward the results I intend to achieve through each of the next day's activities and notice how each imagined result feels in my body.

Over the years of practicing, I have found that I learn even more by listening to all four of my bodies – my mental body, my emotional body, my intuitive body, as well as my physical body. What it means to recapitulate in my physical body is to relive the feeling of the experience as I felt it at the time in my bones, my muscles, my cells; feeling my heartbeat. Feeling what it was like to sit in the chair during the lunch meeting, or hold the phone in my hand during a coaching call. Feeling the experience in my physical body creates a tangible connection with the situation.

To feel the experience in my mental body is to remember what was said and what I thought about what was said at the time and what I think about what was said in the present moment. As I remember with my mental body, I notice that my emotional body reminds me of the emotions I felt during the experience and the emotions I am feeling in the present time. As I notice my emotions change through each re-called experience, I am better able to notice which ones produced positive and energetically uplifting feelings, as well as any that produced energetically draining feelings, such as sadness, disappointment, frustration, etc.

I utilize my intuitive wisdom to bring inner knowingness to each experience.

As I am in the process of recapitulating, I imagine hitting the re-play button on each of the day's activities and I feel what it was like to be participating in the coaching call, or the networking meeting, or dinner with my husband. With all four of my bodies recapitulating at the same time, I have a fuller view of the experience. I am more able to acknowledge myself for what I contributed to and/or learned from the experience.

I am also better able to capture the items I want to add to Side #1 and Side #3 of my Plan, such as any *qualities* I noticed that I liked about the people with whom I interacted during the day. I often have additional **goals** and **intentional activities** to add to my Plan as a result of the day's experiences.

This is also the time when I notice which items on my Plan were fulfilled during the day so that during my *A.P.E.*, I can acknowledge "Yes, I feel like I'm getting closer!"   In recapitulating, I often notice situations where I feel I missed an opportunity, which provides me an opportunity to create a follow-up experience. Or, if it doesn't feel right to follow-up with that specific person again, I can still cast in this way: "If that ever comes up again, I will remember to say X."

Then, I am ready to create my *Appreciation Perspective Experience (A.P.E.)*. Upon completing my acknowledgements of appreciation, I then say,

> *"I've gotten the lessons, I've gotten the information, I've acknowledged what I have attracted, I've squeezed all the juice out of this day's activities. Now, I am empowered to be even more intentional tomorrow!"*

This statement moves me easily into casting the next day– like a net into the waters to capture what we want....or writing and casting myself in a play about how I want the next day to be.

Casting invites me to consider what I'm going to be doing throughout each minute of the next day, and to set my intended results for each **intentional activity** I have already scheduled. While casting, I am able to determine if I have sufficiently prepared for each **activity**, scheduled enough time in-between each **activity** (more about this in Chapter 9), and to notice if there are any other **activities** that I must accomplish the next day that I did not yet put on my calendar. It is also an opportunity to receive the power and support of all four of my bodies...not just my mind in planning the next day.

As I sit quietly and cast the next day, I set an intention for the time I want to wake up in the morning and what I will eat for breakfast and what I plan to wear tomorrow and how much time I'm going to give to feeding and playing with the dogs and how I intend to interact with my husband, Bill, and then the results I intend to achieve from my first appointment. I envision what materials I will prepare to achieve those results. And, I continue to intend the next 24 hours in the same way. I feel the experiences in all four bodies, as if I am living them right now while I am casting. I notice the feelings that each body brings to me and I make adjustments in my intentions to ensure that every one of the feelings is powerfully and positively energized.

As mentioned earlier in this chapter, casting is a "process of warming up the body and introducing it to the themes to come...you have never experienced what will happen tomorrow. Experiment and enjoy." By setting my intention for the results I want to achieve the next day, I have warmed up all four of my bodies to be ready for the day will bring...to support me in getting the rest I need...and to allow me to relax and trust that I am fully empowered to enjoy the next day.

As I share this **Chi-Generating Ritual** with my clients, they report how quickly they are able to break the habit of dwelling over and over again on frustrating aspects of their day, on any mistakes they felt they made, or on what person treated them badly...and waking up with the same negative, energy draining thoughts in their head as they start the next day. Through the process of recapitulation, they learn as I have that we can re-generate ourselves newly each day.

Recapitulation and Casting is the ritual I choose for the evening and prepares me for my morning **Chi-Generating Ritual**; a ritual I created to ensure that I remember the most important thing in the world to me as soon as I open my eyes.

No matter how busy my morning, it takes me just a minute to say,

• • • • • • $\left[\begin{array}{l}\textit{"The most important thing in the} \\ \textit{world to me is to make God smile."}\end{array}\right]$

Next, I ensure that each one of my chakra energy centers* is fully empowered to support me throughout the day. Carolyn L. Mein, D.C., describes chakras as "energy centers found along the midline of the body, extending through the torso both in the front and the back. The 1st Chakra is located around the tailbone and the 7th Chakra at the top of the head, with the rest in between. Emotions are projected and received via the energy transmitted through the chakras. Once emotions are generated or accepted into our energy field, they move through the body via the meridian system which consists of energy channels that feed all the glands, organs and systems. Emotions, like areas of the body, have specific vibrational frequencies and will accumulate in areas with the same frequency.

This is why certain emotions are associated with certain areas of the body, and how the chakras are connected to the meridian system."

I say the name of the chakra and then envision the color associated with that chakra. When I feel the need for even more chi energy to be generated, I also use the affirmations provided by Carolyn L. Mein, D.C., in her book *"Releasing Emotional Patterns with Essential Oils."*[3]

1st Chakra – 'Root' located at Pubic Bone:
Red

> *"I am one with all that is."*

2nd Chakra – 'Creative' located at Bladder:
Orange

> *"I am complete within myself."*

3rd Chakra – 'Solar Plexus' located at Solar Plexus:
Yellow

> *"I am conscious."*

4th Chakra – 'Heart' located at Heart:
Green

> *"I am enough."*

5th Chakra – 'Throat' located at Throat:
Blue

> *"I express."*

6th Chakra – '3rd Eye' located between eyebrows:
Indigo

> *"I know who I am."*

7th Chakra – 'Crown' located at top of head:
Violet

> *"I am one with all that is."*

8th Chakra – 'Star' located 8" above the Crown:
White

> *"It is my intention to return my Body, Mind and Spirit to the point of Perfection"*

Next, I affirm "I am a Doctor of Natural Medicine' (my **B-All**)

Then, I cleanse my body and my aura using a pure essential oil body wash to raise my energetic vibration. Next, I say prayers for those I know who are ill or would like assistance. Then I close my ritual with this statement:

"I am filled with appreciation, I am confident, I am blessed. I am in the flow of my safe, happy, healthy, purposeful, prosperous, joyful, productive, gentle and loving life!"

Chi-To-Be! Master Chi-Generating Rituals

Sandra S.

I used this chakra chart to assist me in my morning ritual.

*I pasted the image into a word document. I then inserted text boxes and put in the notes for my morning and evening ritual, my **B-All** and what is most important to me in the world. I open each chakra from the base root up to the star chakra (white) above my head. I visualize its color, say my statement and move all the way up. I complete it by stating my **B-All**. I am a little fuzzy in the morning so having the chart and everything written down helps me and it does not take that long.*

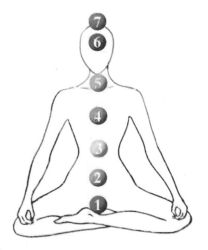

Olivia B.

I have created ritual to allow myself to step into alignment. This is very much like a muscle, the more I do it, the easier it becomes. I participate in ritual that functions as prayer for the earth, for the ways that keep her in harmony with the universe and us, her habitants in harmony with her balance. After every group ritual, no matter its purpose, I repeat my personal ritual to remain clean and clear of any uninvited group consciousness that may have clung to my personal energy. I find when I am properly aligned; the ritual is amplified in its intention.

My current morning ritual includes the following:

-Grounding, aligning myself within the heart of the earth and the heart of the cosmos and with any dream messages

-Breathing to activate my chi

-A balance of the elements

-Tantric exercise that can include any movement tradition depending on the state of my body

-Cleansing my auric field as I cleanse my body.

*-Thanking the universe and my guides for the co-creation and the steps we take towards my **B-All**.*

Corey S.

*- Each morning, while lying in bed, I ground myself and set my intention on what I plan to achieve towards my **B-All** for the day.*

- I give thanks for being here another beautiful day

- I declare all that I am to the universe

- I call upon my Higher Self guides and give appreciation

- I say a few prayers

- At night, I meditate 10-15 minutes before bedtime

Maria J.

I have used the image of a mandala for focus. My B-All mandala has my B-All as its center and the rays emerging from that center are all the different aspects of healing and well-being that my B-All will provide to others.

My daily morning and evening mandala center is gratitude. The rays emerging from it are all the things I am grateful for in my life. It is my meditation. I often choose a word which will become the center of my mandala for the day.

Tara R.

Morning Rituals and Bedtime Rituals have changed my life. As a child, my granny Pearl encouraged me to get up early and read the Bible. As much as I tried reading that Bible daily, I hated and resented it and could not get through Genesis. Also, after having children, the idea of getting up earlier than I have to was VERY unappealing.

In January of this year, I committed to read the entire Bible in a year. I also decided I would read it first thing every morning. It is now the main part of my morning ritual. Today is December 9th. I am almost completely finished. This year has been one of the best, most productive and most challenging years of my life.

My family has encountered huge obstacles, including a 15-year business relationship failing. Yet, I personally feel better, more grounded, more present, more loving and productive than ever. My husband and I are closer than we have ever been in 17 years, I am grateful and excited to greet each day and to see what God is bringing into my life. Now, I have added Recapitulation and Casting at night, and I feel a stronger sense of balance.

Loralee H.

My morning ritual begins with climbing out of bed and going for a run or to the gym to do weights. Then, I'll review in my mind the day's activities before me, including who I need to contact. On mornings that I don't have to immediately go to work, I'll take more time getting up and do a brief meditation.

Evening ritual consists of being with B. to unwind from the day. I go over in my mind what needs to be prepared for the next day, and/or what took place that day. I'll often do a meditation before going to sleep, connect with my guides and Higher Self, requesting help or insight on various things that came up during the day. Often there will be energy running through me, clearing and transforming whatever needs to be done.

Michael T.

*I say my prayers for 10 minutes before getting out of bed. Upon arising, I watch a mind movie and then look at my Strategic Plan. I put on my positive frame of mind and allow myself to relax and shower. I read and write my **goals** and structure my day. I always end with self-levitation, assisted levitation and professional levitation. I do my Transcendental Meditation and start my day.*

In the evening, I do my TM before dinner. I do Lucid dreaming for an hour before bed. Then review my Strategic Plan and watch my mind movie. I am ready to have this work on my unconscious all night. I also keep a dream log for my lucid dreaming.

Christina L.

*I recapitulate by using sense memory, a tool that actors utilize to put themselves physically into past experiences in order to actually smell the smells and feel the feelings of a specific place and time. Sense memory strengthens my ability to visualize and feel the feelings of being my **B-All** throughout my day.*

•••••••••• RECAP ••••••••••

1 A **Chi-Generating Ritual** can be any **intentional activity** you choose to implement daily and/or consistently to bring a Goal, or ultimately a *B-All*, closer to fulfillment...or into being.

2 A **Chi-Generating Ritual** is intended to be the activating and catalyzing force behind every other **intentional activity** undertaken each day.

3 Looking at your **Strategic Attraction Plan™** every day to remain focused on your *B-All* could be considered a **Chi-Generating Ritual.**

4 Practicing your *Appreciation Perspective Experience* (Going *A.P.E.*) every day could be considered a **Chi-Generating Ritual.**

5 The practice of **'Recapitulation and Casting'** is another ritual you may wish to adopt at the end of each day in order to be better prepared to fulfill your intentions for the next day.

6 **Recapitulation** is accomplished by reliving "the experience by sensing it in your body rather than thinking about it."

7 **Casting** is a "process of warming up the body and introducing it to the themes to come."

8 Utilizing **The Four Agreements®** adds power to any
Chi-Generating Ritual.

9 Connecting with your Chakra energy centers is an effective
Chi-Generating Ritual because they are said to be "force
centers" or whorls of energy.

*To learn more about Chakras and their meanings, and for a
variety of articles and website listings on this subject you may
wish to visit:
   http://en.wikipedia.org/wiki/Chakra or
   http://www.experiencefestival.com/meaning_of_chakra

(1) *The American Heritage® Dictionary of the English Language, Fourth
Edition copyright ©2000 by Houghton Mifflin Company. Updated in
2009. Published by Houghton Mifflin Company. All rights reserved*

(2) *Meditations and Rituals Using Aromatherapy Oils by Gill Farrar-
Halls, copyright @2001 by Godsfield Press and Gill Farrer-Halls,
Published by Sterling Publishing Company, Inc.*

(3) *Releasing Emotional Patterns with Essential Oils by Carolyn L. Mein,
D.C., Eighth Edition copyright ©1998 by Carolyn L. Mein, D.C.,
Published by VisionWare Press., http://www.bodytype.com*

chapter 8
Keeping Your Chi Moving

8TH CHI-TO-BE! ENERGY SURGE™

I've long known the importance of maintaining a clear space in which to attract what I desire – a short tip on this Law of Attraction principle was included in *'Attracting Perfect Customers... The Power of Strategic Synchronicity'* (See Chapter 4).

• • • • • • • •
> *However, I truly began to understand that keeping my life and environment free of clutter is vital to keeping my energy vibrating fully when I began learning the principles of Feng Shui.*

Dating back to at least 4000 B.C., the Chinese have oriented their lives around the principles of Feng Shui. Feng Shui means literally Wind-Water and followers believe it is a way of using the laws of both Heaven (astronomy) and Earth (geography) to improve one's life by receiving Chi (or 'qi') and keeping it flowing.

While there are a variety of Feng Shui variations, called 'Sects,' there is a common perspective held that the physical/tangible clutter in our environment is a metaphor for the clutter we have elsewhere in our lives...and that clutter is blocking the flow of Chi energy to and around us.

Symmetry is an important element to maintaining the flow of Chi. Yet, some amount of disorganization can also contribute to keep Chi flowing.

Internationally recognized Feng Shui expert, Terah Kathryn Collins writes about 'Active' and 'Passive' chaos in "Home Design with Feng Shui A-Z."[1] She describes chaos in general as *"part of the cycle of life. Because we cannot live without creating chaos on a regular basis, it's important to understand the two kinds of chaos. Active chaos is the kind of chaos we see spinning around a chef as he prepares a feast, or around a painter as she creates a masterpiece. Active chaos has to occur to birth anything. The key to keeping chaos active is clean up the mess and reorganize our materials between creative bursts. Then, when the next wave of creativity hits, we are ready to dive in.*

A mess left for long becomes passive chaos. We know it's passive chaos when it annoys, confuses, or stops us. There's no lively Chi there, just a big old mess. Passive chaos symbolizes old thoughts and patterns that 'mess up' the quality of your life."

Collins offers these important "Clear The Way" Questions to help clean up passive chaos messes:

1. Do I love it?
2. Do I need it?
3. Does it support who I am now in my life?
4. Does it act as an environmental affirmation for me?
5. What positive and/or negative thoughts, memories, or emotions do I associate it with it?
6. Does it need to be fixed or repaired, and am I willing to do so?
7. If it's time to let it go, am I going to sell, lend, or give it away and when? [1]

Are Your Piles Made of 'Shoulds'?

Consider that the 'stuff' we have lying around, gathering dust, that we keep moving around instead of putting away has a weight to it, and it is easy to understand why the energy of those piles is heavy and draining…rather than light and energizing.

Often, these piles accumulate during periods of time when have an accumulation of 'stuff' clogging up our minds…the 'stuff' that we continually ponder and worry about…without taking action or identifying solutions.

From a Feng Shui stand point, the way to arrive at solutions is to take an action that moves Chi energy. By physically clearing the clutter of physical items, we can also move the clutter out of our minds…in order to see the solutions.

In many ways, clearing the clutter is similar to 'casting' our future. If we want Chi energy to flow in and around us at all times, then it is important to keep our environments clear of all energy blocks.

As we each continue to keep our eye focused on our *B-All*, setting our **goals**, and scheduling **intentional activities**, we can expect to be creating 'Active' chaos. Life is going to become more abundant, not less abundant. So, it is to be expected that clearing clutter will become a regularly scheduled **intentional activity** to avoid any 'Passive' chaos from accumulating.

Often, as my clients begin to attract more and more of what they desire, will complain to me that they 'don't have enough time' to handle all the abundance.

This 'lack of time' usually shows up in their lives first as not having time to read and respond to emails or return phone calls in a timely way. The messages start stacking up along with the 'shoulds' (I 'should' call that person back; I 'should' sit down and answer emails, etc.) and each one of those 'shoulds' has weight to it. Eventually, the joy of abundance is lost and buried under the pile of 'shoulds' and Chi becomes stagnant.

• • • • • • • • • $\left[\begin{array}{c}\textit{Rather than a 'lack of time',}\\ \textit{what they have is an}\\ \textit{abundance of 'shoulds'.}\end{array}\right]$

A long time ago, I read a bumper sticker that stated "Don't Should On Yourself." I took that guidance to heart…and encourage my clients to do the same.

Plan to De-Clutter Daily

I explain to my clients the simplest way to keep the Chi moving is to expect that clearing clutter each day will be a regularly scheduled **intentional activity** from this point forward!

For example, one of my **goals** is to utilize social networking sites and podcasting as effectively as possible to achieve my *B-All*. Each week, I schedule many **intentional activities** towards the fulfillment of this **goal**. One of these **intentional activities** is to read the information I receive via email daily from other people who I consider to already be experts in utilizing social networking and podcasting sites in order to learn how to take these actions myself.

Each day, I receive an abundance of announcements and invitations from people through various social networking sites. In order to keep this information from overwhelming me (and draining my Chi), I schedule a certain amount of time each day to review this information to determine if I want to take immediate action, save it or delete it. I've created Folders on my computer desktop to categorize the items that I want to save for future reference. Once the information is in those Folders, I don't have to think about it again until I am ready to take action on that information. This information and any other invitations on which I will take action are scheduled into my calendar and then flagged in my email system as having been scheduled. Everything else is immediately deleted. I choose how much time I want to give to clearing the clutter each day. Some days it is more and some days less. As long as I am clearing something, I know I am keeping my Chi moving.

Create Your Clutter Clearing Game

Consider this an invitation to make clearing clutter into a game. How many items can you clear everyday with the intention to get your Chi flowing towards achieving your **goals**? Are you willing to schedule 15 minutes each day to clear your clutter? Imagine how much trash can be thrown away – physically or virtually – in just 15 minutes?

What reward or prize will you give to yourself for winning your Clutter Clearing Game?

Many of my clients report back to me that they receive surprise gifts of abundance almost immediately after clearing their clutter. At the end of this chapter, you will hear from the **Chi-To-Be! Masters** as to the many gifts and rewards they received almost magically by playing their own Clutter Clearing Game.

One of the benefits often discovered by clearing clutter is the ability to have more appreciation for what you have…another opportunity to go *A.P.E.* each day!

In the past, I would go to a store every day to buy something new. I was always focused on what I did not have or own already. So, as soon as I had money in my pocket, I went to the store to purchase at least one new thing. This happened almost every day. Then, I learned that I could attract more abundance into my life by clearing clutter.

I started with my closet and asked myself what I was willing to give away in order to be able to attract abundance to buy something better. I noticed that everything in my closet was something I enjoyed wearing and did not want to give away. I already felt more abundant!

I decided instead to throw away paperwork I no longer needed.

Within a day or two of clearing the paperwork clutter, I realized that I felt more satisfied with myself and stopped feeling the urge to shop. I no longer felt that I was lacking in any way. I gave the money I saved as donations to charities instead, which is an **intentional activity** towards my **goal** of creating a charitable foundation.

Now, if I choose to shop for clothes, a home decoration, or any other item, I make it a game to identify something I will give away to charity. As a result of playing this game, I stopped buying clothes that I do not truly need. The money I have saved from not buying clothes has instead been spent on adding to my supply of essential oils. As an element of my Aromatherapy Coaching practice, I share these oils with my clients. This is an **intentional activity** towards my **B-All**, which is "to achieve my doctorate in Natural Medicine and to teach thousands of people around the world how to honor and care for their physical, emotional, mental, and energy bodies before I leave this earth."

Ways to Play

If playing the Clutter Clearing Game is a new **intentional activity** for you, remember that it is ok to play your Game 'poorly' in the beginning. Your **intentional activity** may be to clean up an entire room in 15 minutes and that may not be possible at the beginning. Yet, any action you take towards clearing the clutter in that room during those 15 minutes will make a big difference.

At the same time, it is not necessary to wait until the scheduled Game time to delete or throw-away items. If you see a piece of paper lying around, take a moment to throw that piece of paper away. You can come back to deal with more items later. Even one item removed will get Chi moving.

Also, there are as many ways to de-clutter and remove as many items as possible each day as you can imagine. Here's just a few that I use or have been shared with me by clients:

1. You may want to add the following item to Side #3 of your Attraction Plan, "I keep my Chi flowing every day by clearing clutter." As you write this item on Side #3, I also invite you to notice what other **goals** and **intentional activities** you have written on that Side. Consider, as well, how clearing clutter each day will support you in achieving those **goals** and **intentional activities**. Will clearing the clutter help you to relieve stress? How will the relief of stress support you in achieving your **goals** and **intentional activities**? How will clearing the clutter make space in which to attract more of what you desire?

2. Put a 'Clutter' box in each room of your home. Each time you walk into that room, select an item to be put into the Clutter box until you are ready to file or throw it away.

3. Assign each room in your home or office a day of the week and only de-clutter that room on that particular day.

4. Hire a professional organizer to come into your home and office and help you set up an organizing system that you can then maintain.

5. Tie your Clutter Clearing Game to your daily morning and/or evening ritual to uplift and empower you in the process.

6. Create your Game with a friend and take turns jointly clearing out the clutter in each others' homes and offices. Take one room at a time. If you are in your home, survey the room together and let your friend support you in deciding what you want to keep and want you can give/throw away depending upon how each item feels to you. Also, keep in mind your **B-All**. Does each item serve you in achieving your **B-All** as quickly as possible? If so, keep it. If not, release it and give it away.

I helped a dear friend of mine to do exactly this process after her father passed away and she was responsible for clearing out his home so it could be sold. Since she had so many memories and emotional responses to each item, she felt that she needed me to help her to make the toughest decisions. I supported her by ensuring that the only items she kept were items she truly loved or made her happy and which she would use or display in her home. Everything else had to be put into one of three areas:

---•—•——•——

Area 1: Items to give to relatives

Area 2: Items to be given to charity

Area 3: Items to be put into trash bags and taken to the dump

---•—•——•——

We cleared four decades of memories and emotions in less than 2 days!

Here are a few suggestions of how to de-clutter from the experiences of the **Chi-To-Be! Masters**:

Olivia B.

*"I have de-cluttered my Bedroom closet and Work space. The **goal** I associate with this task is the amount of Family Time I intended for this month. My bedroom closet is a shared space at this point in time since I am not living in my own home. I have found it challenging to keep it looking neat and actually being uncluttered. The work space is consistently cleaned by me once a week and I will take the opportunity to file receipts and get ready for the end-of-the-year organization. Having an organized closet helps me feel organized in my daily energetic space. My office organized allows room for more clients, correspondence and growth, as well as a shared learning space for my daughter who uses it as well. I like to feel prepared so choosing these spaces has helped me to feel ready for the reality of the monthly **goals** I'm achieving and better preparing me for the Chi to flow right in to empower next month's **goals**. I can tell because they are already making their presence known."*

Corey S.

"I have a tendency to put papers and other materials I plan to read in one big pile on my desk. The reality is that that pile will not get read until I de-clutter my whole desk. Today, I read many of them. The information I absorbed was worth the effort. Moving forward, though, I will no longer put things in a pile for later, because some of this information would have been beneficial to know a few weeks ago. De-cluttering my workspace allows me to be more focused on the task at hand. I also feel like it allows thoughts to flow more freely, and brings a sense of peace and ease to my being."

Lauren K.

"I cleaned out all the clutter from the spare bedroom in my apartment. This aligned with my **goal** *in completely releasing an ex-boyfriend out of my life, who was previously living with me. One of our mutual friends picked up all of my ex's stuff and then I threw out the rest of the things he had given me that I did not want to keep. I noticed the energy in my entire apartment change once his belongings were removed. Clearing the clutter was extremely therapeutic and is helping me move forward in achieving all of* **goals** *and my* **B-All**. *I feel so much more free and liberated. I found one last small item of his in a drawer last night and it felt incredibly empowering to throw it down the trash chute."*

Michael T.

*"I have partially cleaned out my closets, and will continue to do so. I am also cleaning my desk where I do most of my work and realigning my office with everything in its proper place and to eliminate anything I have not used in 6 months. This will free up my energy and allow the new to come in. I am also cleaning my mind and using "The 4 Agreements"*ᴿᵀᴹ. *The result has been two new clients. By avoiding making assumptions and doing my best, I allowed that space of freedom and positive energy to carry me forward."*

Sandra S.

One of my **goals** *is to build a strong physical body that supports my* **B-All** *and supporting* **goals** *by building my strength and energy. A few of my intentional activities to achieve this* **goal** *are: to walk 30 minutes every day, add one healthful food a week, eliminate one bad food and use weights three times a week. I noticed that I have not been able to take a decent amount of time for lunch at work. To that end I have been cleaning and organizing my desk area so that I can see what I need to do in the most efficient way. I noticed the clutter in general has kept me feeling more overwhelmed, and stressful. It is visually distracting. Because I have felt overwhelmed, instead of taking a lunch and walking around to relieve stress, I have just let the clutter envelop me. As such, I have also been not following up on things in my new job and life. As an example, I let lapse 3 domains in my name that I have had for ten years. To get them back will now cost me $300. I am also tired and feel emotionally down and stagnant. This is how the clutter blocks my mastery and growth. This weekend I plan to take my laundry out to be done, clean the bathroom and take care of my personal needs by getting a haircut and possibly my nails, too."*

Christina L.

> *"I fulfilled one of my* **goals** *this week by moving into my new home. I have thrown out half of the things I owned — clothing, old files, gave away a ton of bags that I never used. I threw away 3 bags full of old food in the refrigerator and completely cleaned it out. As I was doing laundry, I found more clothes I never wear. Now, I am constantly looking for things to throw out at my house and others' homes (LOL)!!! I clean out my car every day at the gas station because I can't stand clutter any more. My room is spotless and waiting for me when I get home with all of my clothes arranged neatly. I look forward to continuing to live clutter free inside and out."*

 Valerie M.

> *"I focused on my* **goal** *of setting up my new office. I am in the* **BLOOMING** *stage with this* **goal***, and it was the perfect time for de-cluttering. I felt like I was weeding my beautiful garden. I purchased a very useful desk for my sewing machines. That is the only item I added to the room. Otherwise, I enjoyed moving things out. I set up my files and threw away tons of paper clutter. Now, my room feels inviting. It feels like a place where I can focus and accomplish a lot. I already feel accomplished! I am noticing that the peace I feel in my office is continuing into other rooms, as well. I have been adding to my 'give-away bag' every day. My bedroom is back to being a peaceful sanctuary and I am even thinking of rearranging the furniture for a new flow of energy. This* **activity** *towards one* **goal** *is helping me achieve another* **goal***, as well. I desire to create more balance in my life. I will feel more balanced when I am taking time to write, do art, exercise and do yoga. Now that my room is de-cluttered and arranged, I can easily spend a little time each day doing my balancing activities. What a wonderful gift!"*

DeZ O.

"The most important thing in the world that is so precious to me is the power of love and how it empowers me. Love has as many different beautiful facets as a beautiful diamond. With that in mind, I woke up one morning thinking, 'my bedroom is the heart of where I receive my most profound messages during meditations, it is where I go to chat on the phone with my friends in private, it is where I go to recharge my own energy, it is where I do most of my distant healing session, and it where I daydream of my perfect soul mate and romance! This is the most sacred space within my home for me.' I literally jumped out of bed and looked around realizing that my bedroom had become more of a storage room. That just won't do anymore folks. I felt like an inspired Artist clearing her canvas of work she no longer was inspired to finished, and letting Spirit move me where to begin this new creation. Just that quick, even though I had not moved one thing, the energy of the room shifted. I guess I got the attention of my Beloved Guides and they approved. I may have to bribe my son to help move some stuff out to the garage, but I'm sure I can think of something... FOOD! In addition to deciding to de-clutter my bedroom, I also set a **goal** *to de-clutter my old website so that it represents the new energy of 'Serenity Living Wellness.' The surprise result is this: I was blessed by my incredible parents with a gift of a new laptop. My personal 'sacred room is where I will go to connect with my 'creative guides' to feel like Picasso in creating future projects on my new laptop. That is sweet!"*

A De-Cluttering Affirmation

Feng Shui expert, Terah Kathryn Collins, author of "Home Design with Feng Shui A-Z", offers the following affirmation to support the process of cleaning up passive chaos: *"I clear and clean my body, heart, and soul, knowing that the more I let go of the old, the more I attract new, inspiring, enjoyable people, places, and things into my life! I trust that all of my needs are met as they arise all the time."*[1]

Consider the concept that our bodies are the temples that house our true spirits. With this in mind, I invite you to utilize Terah Kathryn Collins' affirmation as a meditation to go beyond simply de-cluttering your home, office and other physical environments to discover what it means to you to 'clear and clean' your 'body, heart, and soul' to attract 'new, inspiring, and enjoyable people, places and things' into your life.

When I embraced the concept that my body is a temple and began to meditate upon how to keep it as clean and pristine as possible, I attracted to me each of the Chi-generating energy surges that I share throughout this book…as well as many more methods and techniques I now practice daily to release stale, old and blocked emotional and mental energy for greater whole-body wellness.

This practice has supported me to continually identify ways to take even better care of my 'temple' in every way. In doing so, I increasingly attract a larger number of supportive, inspiring and enjoyable people into my life … people who also honor, respect and continuously de-clutter their 'temple,' too.

These additional methods and techniques are shared and practiced with those who participate in the **Chi-To-Be! Mastery Coaching Program**. Turn to Chapter 13 for more information about this program, which is designed to support you in keeping your physical, mental, and emotional space open, clear, harmonized, balanced and powerfully generating active energy.

• • • • • • • • • • RECAP • • • • • • • • • •

1 A common perspective of Feng Shui is the 'physical/tangible clutter in our environment' is a metaphor for the clutter we have elsewhere in our lives…and that clutter is blocking the flow of Chi energy to and around us.

2 Most clutter is made of 'shoulds' or things we think we 'should do' or feel an obligation to do, which is why they collect in piles instead of getting done or completed.

3 To keep Chi moving, plan to de-clutter by removing as many items as possible from your home or office every day.

4 Creating a Clearing Clutter Game makes the process more fun, which automatically provides uplifting and energizing Chi!

5 Add, "I keep my Chi flowing every day by clearing clutter" to Side #3 of your Attraction Plan to keep the process connected to the fulfillment of your **B-All.**

6 Turn to Chapter 13 to learn more about the **Chi-To-Be!™ Mastery Coaching Program** and how it may support you in keeping your physical, mental, and emotional space open, clear, harmonized, balanced and powerfully generating active energy.

(1) *"Home Design with Feng Shui A-Z" by Terah Kathryn Collins, copyright ©1999 Terah Kathryn Collins, published by Hay House, Inc., P.O. Box 5100, Carlsbad, CA 92018-5100, 800/654-5125.*

CHI-TO-BEI

chapter 9
Re-charging Your Inner Chi

9TH CHI-TO-BE! ENERGY SURGE™

As we first explored in Chapter 3, there will be times when our **goal(s)** are at **rest** because they have been completed or are no longer providing energy towards achieving your *B-All*.

However, while a **goal** is still in development through the stages of *Seeding*, *Sprouting*, and *BLOOMING*, it is important to schedule in time to **rest** as an **intentional activity** to re-charge our inner Chi batteries – to clear space internally – so to speak.

Scheduling a **rest stop** is a conscious practice of rejuvenation. It's a proactive pause in the **activity** to catch one's breath and to ensure there is a balance between action and non-action.

Our morning and evening rituals are an opportunity each day to take this time. Yet, taking an entire day, a full week, or even a month…or longer…to give our minds and bodies a **rest** from a particular project or challenge can actually be much more productive and enjoyable than continuously focusing our energy on the issue.

> How will you know when to continue to focus and when it's time to schedule a **rest stop**?

The answer is quite simple…as long as you feel you are 'in the flow' of the project and you are making progress, continue to put your energy into the project. At the point at which you notice that you no longer feel energized when you think about the project…that's the time to implement a **rest stop**.

I learned this principle on a physical level six years ago when I first began learning Nia Technique routines with the **goal** of teaching classes to help others develop greater wellness through movement. Learning the routines was my first **intentional activity** towards achieving my **goal**. I scheduled a set time each day for this **intentional activity** and I expected that each time I practiced my first routine I would feel more comfortable in my movements. I also expected that I would keep practicing the same routine over and over again daily until I perfected teaching it before moving on to the next routine to learn on my list.

What I did not expect is that I would come to a point in my practice that I simply could not stand to practice the routine one more time!

I began to dread the approach of my practice time. The thought of listening to the music one more time literally made my ears ache. My joy for experiencing Nia was diminishing quickly….along with my passion for achieving my **goal**.

> *One day, I took a* **rest stop** *from practicing.*

During that day, a new **intentional activity** came to my mind. I considered that rather than waiting until I finished learning the first routine, I could begin to listen to the music for the second routine I wanted to learn while I was driving to appointments and running errands. In this way, I would become familiar with it before beginning to practice the actual routine, which would move me forward with velocity towards my **goal** of teaching NIA classes.

I began to play the new CD and found that I truly loved the music. My body naturally and easily moved to the music…even while driving! I became curious as to the movements of the routine. The next day, instead of pushing myself to practice the first routine, I played the DVD for the second routine. I loved it! I found my body easily took to the movements and I became comfortable in teaching the second routine very quickly. My joy for Nia was full and present and alive again!

Now that I had a learned a full routine, I was ready to attract a Nia class to teach. That, too, happened very quickly. The teacher of the class that I was attending as a student announced at our next class that she would be moving to another state within the month. I applied for the position, was accepted, and stepped in easily to teach her class. I have been teaching NIA classes every week since for the past six years.

Let's go back to the first routine I was learning. Now that I had fully learned and was teaching the second routine, I felt ready to finish learning the first routine. I was amazed that when I returned to practicing that first routine, the movements seemed much easier to me. I felt as if I 'understood' the routine for the very first time. I fell back in love with the music. Within a very short amount of time, I now had two routines I felt comfortable teaching.

I believe that the **rest stop** I took and the resulting decision to switch to a routine with music I enjoyed served me in a variety of ways, two of which are:

1. By beginning with movements that were easier for my body to learn, I was able to exercise and condition my body to a greater degree...which made it possible for me to then learn a more difficult routine with greater ease.

2. By completing an **intentional activity**, which led directly to the fulfillment of my **Goal**, I was empowered to keep my **goal** in continuous action. Since that time, I continue to learn my routines in this way. I practice one until I feel that I have squeezed all the joy out of it and then I take a **rest stop** from that routine and begin to practice another one that is quite different in movement and music mood. I find that by balancing the two, I learn both routines much quicker and with more energy than I would if I continued to keep forcing myself to learn the first one by itself.

I later learned that I had tapped into the balance of yin and yang.

The Yin and Yang of Chi

The Yin/Yang symbol is created by two flowing circles with a smaller circle of Yin inside the Yang, and a smaller circle inside the Yin. The circles are believed to represent the circular nature of the philosophy and symbolize that one extreme will always change into its opposite. In other  words, extreme yang will turn into yin and vice versa...similar to day turning into night and night turning into day.

To distinguish between the two, according to Chinese philosophy, it is important to understand the traits associated with each one. Yang is associated with day, extroversion, masculine, sun, and **activity**. Yin is associated with the opposite traits of introversion, feminine, moon, and **rest**. Of course, nothing in the universe is completely yin or completely yang.

So, if we are always feeling that we must be on the 'go, go, go' and not giving ourselves enough time to '**rest, rest, rest**,' our Chi will become imbalanced leading to difficulties and challenges which will require us to stop and **rest**. This is why it is believed that too much yang within one's self will lead to illness... requiring more **rest** (yin).

The same is true if we put too much attention on any of our **goal(s)** without giving sufficient time to take a **rest** from focusing on the **goal(s)**. Eventually, our energy, ideas, and resources will be exhausted requiring us to stop any way... .perhaps for a much longer period of time than would have been required if short **rest stops** were taken along the way.

As you can probably tell, I tend to be more yang than yin in the way I approach life.

For example, in the past, when preparing to go on vacation, I would invest a lot of energy in completing all my projects before I left so that I would not have to think about them while I was on vacation. This usually meant long hours and improper nutrition to meet my self-imposed deadlines. So, what always happened as soon as I stopped to enjoy my vacation? Of course, I got sick! I have had to learn to embrace the yin and trust that my **rest stops** and vacations are opportunities for my mind to clear out the clutter to be able to see the project or **goal** even more clearly and creatively. By waiting to complete some of my **intentional**

activities towards my **goal** until after a **rest stops** – which includes getting sufficient sleep and nourishing food, exercise, vitamins and minerals – I always experience a renewed and increased flow of joyful energy which produces greater results than would be possible by pushing myself to an 'unnatural' finish line.

Of course, this requires proper planning in advance…and sometimes it also requires having to re-negotiate agreements with others when I see that I may have miscalculated the amount of time required to complete a project or achieve a **goal**.

This is why it is important for me to schedule each **intentional activity** towards the **goal** in advance in order to determine a reasonable amount of time to complete each one.

It is also requires my willingness to plan poorly at first until the amount of time required becomes more predictable…along with my commitment to do my best in each moment…whether I am doing or I am **resting**.

I invite you now to take a moment to consider if your approach to life is more yin, more yang, or a balance between the two. Do you schedule regular **rest stops** each day or do you delay your breaks until a project or **goal** is obtained?

Even Music Takes Rest Stops!

Another way of looking at the importance of taking **rest stop** is to consider how **rest periods** are used in music. Take a moment now to listen to your favorite song. Listen to the rhythm, the melody, the phrasing of how the song is composed. Notice each beat and instrument. And, notice when each instrument **rests**. It is these **rest periods** that actually create the mood of the music.

Without the **rest periods**, all there would be is beat, beat, beat, beat, beat, beat, beat, beat, etc. Together, the beats and the **rest periods** create what is known as music. So, without the silence, there is no music; there's only noise.

Chi-To-Be! Master Valerie M. shares:

Valerie M.

> *"As a stay-at-home mother of two toddlers, and another one on the way, I can easily forget about the* **rest stops**. *Lately, I have been waking up to a quiet home before the kids begin their day. I have celebrated those moments in between, when no one else is awake and I am left to my own energy, intentions and thoughts. My husband is a professional musician and he jokes of being paid by the note....I can appreciate the value of the notes between for it makes it possible for the notes played out loud to have their true meaning. Like the shallow brook who babbled most, the opposite is always recognized."*

Resting is Re-charging!

If we desire to create a harmonious life for ourselves....there must be time to sit in silence, to **rest**, to listen to both our own intuition and to Divine inspirations.

Chi-To-Be! Master Maria J. feels

Maria J.

> *"****Resting*** *is as important as breathing. I used to think that* ***Resting*** *meant escaping; not recharging. I now know that learning to recharge is learning to do activities which heal me."*

For most of us, it may not be necessary or possible to **rest** for long periods of time. That's why it is important to plan even short spaces of time in-between appointments and other activities each day.

Chi-To-Be! Master Tara R. inserts 15-minute **rest stops** into her day in this way:

Tara R.

"I have utilized a technique for **resting** *for more than 20 years. It really isn't sleep or meditation. I call it un-plugging for 15 minutes — 5 minutes to calm, 5 minutes to just 'Be,' 5 minutes to return to my day. It's simple, yet key, in caring for myself and sustains my energy throughout the day. I can really feel a difference at the end of a day when I haven't done this for myself."*

Chi-To-Be! Master Loralee H. is now practicing implementing **rest stops** in-between her client appointments.

Loralee H.

"Spaces of nothing have been few this year for me. I'm definitely feeling the need for more. Last Friday, after I finished running in the park, I sat and watched the full moon rise over the small lake, heard the night animals rustling around, and had a skunk come up and sniff my foot, checking me out....a very nice quiet moment. Another Chi re-charging moment occurred a few days ago. I was feeling very tired and low on energy. I had some time in between clients, and knowing I wasn't in a position where I could nourish myself, I did a meditation that really helped boost my energy which helped me get through the rest of the day. It's something I'll definitely use again. **Rests** *between the notes are definitely something I now cherish!"*

Chi-To-Be! Master Lauren K. confirms the importance of taking short **rest** breaks in-between **activities**.

Lauren K.

"This week I did not give myself much time to relax or do nothing. I plan on scheduling more time to do nothing and give myself more breaks within my schedule. However, when I was playing poker on-line, I would go out on the balcony during the 5-minute break to enjoy the peace and quiet and observe the hectic, fast-paced energy swirling around the Las Vegas Strip casinos. I found it to be extremely refreshing after spending so many long hours at the computer – sitting in peace, as an observer. I have also been smelling my essential oils everyday when I wake up and go to bed; allowing myself a few seconds to take in the smell and enjoy them. I have always been sensitive to smells and creating time to do this in my day makes me happy."

And, Chi-To-Be! Master Olivia B. shares:

Olivia B.

*"I have been reading in my 'quiet me' time and I know this is still 'doing.' So, I have been placing my bare feet on the grass in the backyard to let in the energy of the earth. This not only relaxes me physiologically, it connects me spiritually and I realize I use every non-doing moment to clean my energetic bodies or meditate into stillness. I guess I am still 'doing' in those **rest** moments, though it feels rejuvenating and inspiring as well."*

Planning To Rest and Resting To Plan

As our Attraction Plans attract to us more and more of what we desire, our lives become filled with an abundance of people we enjoy and an ever-expanding amount of activities that we intend to accomplish towards our *B-All*. This is the time when it is even more important to schedule **rest stops** in-between each **activity** so that your life is a beautiful composition of Chi energy in balance.

To create life as a beautiful masterpiece requires planning ahead by remembering that every **intentional activity** – every meeting, every search on the Internet, and every interaction – will produce a result which will require another **intentional activity** to be scheduled.

You may wish to keep your Plan with you throughout the day, so that during short **rest stops** and in-between your **activities**, you can add your new **intentional activities** to Side #3 of your Plan.

In my experience, this method of using **rest stops** as both opportunities to re-charge my batteries as well as to add items to my Plan throughout the day is a much more energizing and balanced practice than waiting to schedule these **activities** until the end of a full day of 'do, do, do's' when I am most likely to be tired and feeling overwhelmed.

Chi-To-Be! Master Christina L. demonstrates how to keep your eye on the *B-All* even while taking a **rest stop**:

Christina L.

"Last week I took a trip to Arizona and enjoyed the art galleries, exploring the desert, enjoying nice dinners, and relaxing at a beautiful resort with some friends. I only played poker 3 days last week and just took time to reflect every night. I actually had a Raindrop Technique® essential oil experience, which was really great and helped me to focus on the growth in my game - not just pushing the **goals** *- a little earth with some fire."*

Chi-To-Be! Master Sandra S. began her practice by implementing a **rest stop** at the end of the day and found that she was doing it poorly at first. She reports,

Sandra S.

"Doing nothing is not the same as re-charging my Chi. I found out that TV watching is not re-charging my Chi. I found it difficult to create useful space for myself. Even though felt I had retreated and was quiet, the space was not created to rejuvenate. The end result is that I have felt very tired. I fall right asleep before I have done my evening ritual."

I expect you will agree that being physically, emotionally, and mentally drained is not the best time to be prioritizing and scheduling your life-fulfilling activities. Remember, each of your **intentional activities** is a priceless opportunity to move forward as quickly as possible towards your *B-All*.

And each **intentional activity** deserves its own **rest stop** – before and after – so that its own results and lessons can be recognized, acknowledged and utilized for empowerment before investing energy in the next one on your path towards fulfilling each and every **goal**.

•••••••••• RECAP ••••••••••

1 There will be times when our **goal(s)** are at **rest**. This is because they have been achieved or they no longer have the power to move us toward our **B-All**.

2 While our **goals** are in the **Seeding**, **Sprouting**, and **BLOOMING** stages, it is important to make the time to **rest** and re-energize before we can implement more intentional activities.

3 **Resting** is a conscious practice of rejuvenation. It's a proactive pause in the **activity** to catch one's breath and to ensure there is a balance between action and non-action.

4 When you are feeling that you have been on the 'go, go, go' and not giving yourself enough time to '**rest, rest, rest**,' your Chi will become imbalanced leading to difficulties and challenges which will require you to stop and **rest**. This is why it is believed that too much yang within one's self will lead to illness…requiring more **rest** (yin).

5 Consider if your approach to life is more yin, more yang, or a balance between the two. Do you schedule regular **rest stops** each day or do you delay your breaks until a project or **goal** is obtained?

6 Listen to your favorite song and notice the rhythm, the melody, the phrasing of how the song is composed. Notice each beat and instrument. And, notice when each instrument

rests. It is these **rest periods** that actually create the mood of the music. Without the **rest periods**, all there would be is beat, beat, beat, beat, beat, beat, beat, beat, etc. Without the silence, there is no music; there's only noise.

7 Schedule **rest stops** in-between each **activity** so that your life is a beautiful composition of Chi energy in balance... have fun, do something completely un-related to the task at hand, or just quietly reflect on your day and what you want to do next.

CHI-TO-BEI

chapter 10
The Solution To Know
What To Do Every Time!

10TH CHI-TO-BE! ENERGY SURGE™

As we come to the next to the last of the **Chi-To-Be! Energy Surges**, I'm going to let you in on a little secret.

• • • • • • • •
> *The fastest way to achieve your B-All with ease is to make the most empowering decisions and choices as quickly as possible each and every time a decision or a choice arises.*

I believe that the reason most people never do achieve their ultimate *B-All* is because a decision or a choice arises while they are achieving more or one of their **goals** and they are unable to identify a solution. They stop to **rest** and reflect, yet the longer they dwell on their choices, the more confused they become. The more confused they become, the more their energy is tied up in the confusion.

In an attempt to release themselves from their confusion, they begin to ask others these 4 automatically dis-empowering words:

"What Should I Do?

Yes, '**automatically dis-empowering!**'

The accepted definition of the word 'should' is to take an action from a sense of obligation or duty.

I believe you will agree with me that it feels far more energizing and empowering to take an action from a sense of desire, passion, commitment, and/or intention.

In addition, when we ask someone else to tell us what to do, we have abdicated our own power – our own inner-knowingness – our own ultimate wisdom.

Asking someone else to tell me what to do has always been my fearful, lazy, wimpy way out of making a decision.

I now know that the only time I do ask someone else for their input is when I have forgotten that I already made a powerfully strong commitment to achieving my *B-All*. In those moments, somehow something else got my attention.

However, once I remember my *B-All* I am completely empowered to make the decision on my own that will move me forward towards its achievement with greater velocity.

I also know that as I continue to implement **intentional activities** from my Plan and I continue to attract more of what I desire, I will attract more and more decisions that will have to be made.

Each of these decisions has the power to also be an energy boost for achieving my **goals**.

For example,
Will I stay in tonight to cuddle with my husband or will I go with my girlfriends to see the movie I have wanted to see with them?

On Side #3 of my Plan, I have written that I expect to spend time with my husband as a balance to my work. I have also written that I expect to spend time with my girlfriends, also as a balance to my work. Which one do I choose in the moment?

Sometimes, I must decide between what appear to be two personally important choices:
I am feeling under-the-weather and my body could use a **rest**. *Yet, my aunt died unexpectedly the day before. Her funeral is tomorrow in another state. I was close to my aunt and would like to be there to pay my respects. Do I go to the funeral?*

This is an actual decision I had to make.

At other times, I may have to choose between two options related to business, such as:
A client, who is dealing with a major health crisis, would like me to facilitate their essential oil anointing session. However, they tell me they are not able to provide my suggested donation fee for this service due to their other medical expenses. I would like to be generous and gift this service to them, yet I also have expenses that must be paid.

Will I be moving closer to or further away from my *B-All* if I choose to accept their request to receive a free oil anointing session?

There have been times, when I am **Recapitulating and Casting** during my **Chi Generating Energy Ritual,** that I realized I forgot to put an **intentional activity** on my calendar and I double-booked myself. How do I decide which **activity** to keep and which **activity** I will re-schedule?

The answer to all of these questions and decisions is the **'Chi-To-Be! Solution Process'** which I created to assist me in making decisions that will move me closer to my *B-All*. The 4-question **'Chi-To-Be! Solution Process'** is simple and quick and provides access to the 'right' answer every time for every type of decision. It is my joy to share this Process with you here.

Is it Love or is it Fear?

Most, if not all, spiritual belief systems are based on the concept that the two most powerful energies are 'love' and 'fear.'

Love is the harmonizing empowering force of nature while Fear is the exact opposite. Fear generates anger, frustration, confusion, agitation, and dis-harmony.

Therefore, decisions made from Love will be quite different than those based on Fear. I believe that if we look at whatever decisions we make at any given time consciously or unconsciously the decision is either made from Love or it's made from Fear.

You may wish to take a moment now to consider a decision you made recently. Did you base your decision on the principle of Love or was your decision generated from Fear?

While writing this book, I faced a decision directly related to one of the key **goals** of my *B-All*

My decision: Whether or not to ask for an extension in submitting the first draft of this book.

Here is how I applied the 4 questions of the **'Chi-To-Be! Solution Process** to arrive at an empowering decision:

Question #1:

Coming from Fear, why would I not ask for an extension?
I don't want to appear unreliable. I am concerned that the publisher will not want to publish the book if the first draft is not provided on time.

Question #2:

Coming from Love, why would I not ask for an extension?
If I am giving Love to my publisher, then I want to be sure I don't delay their plans for the book. If I am giving Love to me, I would not ask for an extension because I want to be seen as reliable and able to keep my word.

Question #3:

Coming from Fear, why would I ask for an extension?
I am concerned that what I have written is not good enough to submit.

Question #4:

Coming from Love, why would I ask for an extension?
If I am giving Love to my publisher, I want to be sure that what I submit is worthy of being published. Asking for an extension now provides sufficient notice and is the most loving action I can take. In this way, the publisher is prepared to give attention to other projects and can co-create with me a new deadline that works for us both. If I am giving Love to me, an extension would give me the time to submit a draft that I truly feel is my best work without extra pressure.. This allows me to write in a relaxed and joyful way...which is what is most empowering for both me and the publisher.

┌─────────────────────────────┐
MY DECISION:
To come from Love and
request an extension.
└─────────────────────────────┘

My Intentional Activity:

*I called the publisher and was granted an extension. In
fact, the extension caused absolutely no problem in the
publisher's schedule due to other projects that were being
given attention at the time.*

I offer you another example of working with the 4 questions
which transpired during a session with a client. The client's
decision was whether or not to continue to take continuing
education classes.

I first asked my client to take a few deep, cleansing breaths to
begin to get her chi flowing. I also asked my client to let go of
any mental distractions and focus only on the Process.

Here is how we moved through the Process:

**S.H.: Coming from Fear, why would you not continue
to take continuing education classes?**

Client: I'm afraid I'll run out of time. I will over-commit myself.

**S.H.: Coming from Love, why would you not continue
to take continuing education classes?**

*Client: Out of love for me, it would be because it doesn't feel like it's
the right time to take any more classes right now.*

S.H.: Coming from Fear, why would you take more continuing education classes right now?

Client: I am afraid of looking foolish to my boss, who is the person who encouraged me to take the classes in the first place.

S.H.: Any other fears you have that would motivate you to take the classes?

Client: Because I think I should be taking them. I know what I can accomplish if I do finish them.

S.H.: Coming from Love, why would you continue to take the continuing education classes?

Client: To continue to educate and stretch myself.

S.H.: Are there any other reasons?

Client: Because I do love the subject. I enjoy taking classes, and I am excited about what I can accomplish when I do finish the classes.

S.H.: As you were going through the Process which one question gave you the best feeling response?

Client: I felt best speaking about both the question out of love for not continuing to take classes by acknowledging that this isn't the right time. I also had a smile on my face when I was responding out of love that I will take more classes to continue to stretch myself and gain more education.

S.H.: So which answer would you say is most empowering for you?

Client: I have to say out of love I won't take the class to honor my feeling that this is not the right time for me to do so.

S.H.: Does that feel like the right decision for you?

Client: It does. And, yet my mind has more questions. I am wondering: if everybody just honored themselves and decided that it wasn't the right time to do something that would be helpful and beneficial, where would we all be?

S.H.: Is that a fear?

Client: It's a judgment. I'm not sure if it's a fear.

S.H.: Well, let's look. What is motivating you to ask the question?

Client: Then, it's a fear, I guess, of what will happen.

S.H.: A fear of what will happen when?

Client: A fear what will happen if I don't continue to do all that I possibly can and my best.

S.H.: I hear that as another fear as to why you would continue to take the classes.

Client: Yes, that's true. Thank you.

S.H.: So now, which one feels more powerful to you? Choosing from fear to continue to take the classes or choosing from love that you would not continue to take classes?

Client: Choosing from love, I will not attend any more classes.

S.H.: And why is that the most powerful answer for you?

Client: Because it does let me say I love the subject matter, and, it's not the right time to take more classes. I know there will be other opportunities. That's my final decision.

I expect that you can clearly hear my client tapping into her power a little more each time she answered the question until she was fully empowered to make her decision.

The **Chi-To-Be! Masters** use the Process as their decision-making tool. Here's a few of their insights and experiences…

Lauren K. used the Process to determine:
Whether or not I should play the 5k Shootout

Question #1:
Coming from Fear, why would I not play the 5k shootout?
I don't want to look bad on camera if I do not play well. Also, the field is extremely tough and I do not want to feel outclassed.

Question #2:
Coming from Love, why would I not play the 5k shootout?
I care about my backer and don't want him to be disappointed in me and want him to realize that I am profitable in live tournaments, so if I don't do well I want him to still put me in live events and believe in me.

Question #3::

Coming from Fear, why would I play the 5k shootout?
If I do not play I am missing out on an invited
opportunity from a potential sponsor and this is a
huge opportunity for me. I can be on ESPN and
if I win, I am almost guaranteed to get a deal and
respect amongst the community.

Question #4::

Coming from Love, why would I play the 5k shootout?
I truly believe this is a great opportunity and it is a
huge sign that one of the employees from
PokerStars™ came up and asked me personally to
play. The opportunity to be on television and be
at a final table as a result of beating only eight
other people at my table is something so easily
achievable, it seems silly for me to not play.

MY DECISION:
Coming from love and playing the 5k shootout

My Intentional Activity:

*I asked my backer to put me in and he agreed. I ended up
playing it and, although I was not in the right mental state, I still
got some television time. Playing was a great opportunity and I
made connections with someone from PokerStars™.*

Olivia B.'s Decision:

Whether or not to aspire for a certificate of aromatherapy?

Question #1:

Coming from Fear, why would I not aspire for a certificate in aromatherapy?
I may not believe in the instructor as an expert.
I may not have enough money to pay for it.
I'm concerned that there will not be a financial payback.

Question #2:

Coming from Love, why would I not aspire for a certificate in aromatherapy?
Because I feel like I am enough and I am on my path with clarity. My specialty is not necessarily clinically-centered and I have no desire to spend money on a piece of official paper. I prefer to focus my attention on under-served communities and my family.

Question #3:

Coming from Fear why would I aspire for a certificate in aromatherapy?
The fear is that I am not enough or that I will not be taken seriously enough by the community without getting certificates to prove my education.

Question #4:

Coming from Love why would I aspire for a certificate in aromatherapy?

To get more education to share with the many who seek it. To improve my own curriculum and create more opportunities for teaching, which I love to do; also to meet new members of the aromatherapy community.

> **MY DECISION:**
> *To not aspire for certification; it is not the focus I have chosen for this stage of my life.*

My Intentional Activity:

*I have contacted someone who I respect as an expert teacher in the field to learn more clinical information so that I can still enhance my curriculum without changing my focus towards my **B-All**. The result is that I feel good about where I am, that I am enough and my* **goals** *are heart-centered and enough as well.*

. . . .

Michael T. also questioned

Whether or not to continue with his education at this time?

Question #1:

Coming from Fear, why would I not stop educating myself with credentials and just do my business?

I am always in fear that I do not know enough of what I need to know and do.

Question #2:

Coming from Love, why would I not stop educating myself with credentials and just do my business?
I love learning and my **goal** is to gain mastery in everything I do.

Question #3:

Coming from Fear, why would I stop educating myself with credentials and just do my business?
Because I have a passion for learning, I never seem to think what tools I have are already good enough.

Question #4:

Coming from Love, why would I stop educating myself with credential and just do my business?
I love to learn. By continuing my education, I am building a huge foundation for my future. More education also builds my confidence. I believe this truth: "The deeper you build, the higher you go up."

> **MY DECISION:**
> *To continue my education and to do my business at the same time.*

My Intentional Activity:

To remember there are no limitations in my life. Freeing!

Tara R. was attracted to the **Chi-To-Be! Masters** Program at one of the busiest times in her life. Her decision was
Whether or not to say 'yes' to herself to participate?

Question #1:

Coming from Fear, why would I not say yes to taking part in the **Chi-To-Be! Masters Coaching Program?** Fear of becoming overwhelmed with "to do's", which stresses out me and my family. I could appear as a "flake" for agreeing and then not being able to catch up/keep up and contribute to the deadlines.

Question #2:

Coming from Love, why would I not say yes to taking part in the **Chi-To-Be! Masters Coaching Program?** Because I love my family and know I am no good to anyone or anything when I am in a state of overwhelm. If I cannot contribute with full attention and respect, then it would be more respectful to say no at this time.

Question #3:

Coming from Fear, why would I take part in the **Chi-To-Be! Masters Coaching Program?** Accepting from Fear that I would be missing not only a wonderful opportunity God has put right into my lap, but also missing an opportunity that provides EXACTLY the tools I've needed to achieve my **goals**. I've been missing the answer to "How do I....?"

Question #4:

Coming from Love, why would I take part in the **Chi-To-Be! Masters Coaching Program?** Because I am learning to trust God's hand in my life; I am learning to feel His Love and guidance in my gut. I am learning to see the incredible clues/opportunities unfold in front of my eyes. That is what happened here. These words appeared in my mind's eye: "Why Not?" and "Love." I felt contrary to my 'logical' sense that by accepting this invitation I would receive and give blessings very important to achieving my *B-All*.

> ### MY DECISION:
> *To participate in the* **Chi-To-Be! Masters Coaching Program**

My Intentional Activity:

Taking part will help me on both my career and personal levels, as well as giving me an opportunity to offer the blessing of sharing my experiences. WIN:WIN!

After more than a year of participation in the **Chi-To-Be! Masters Coaching Program**, Sandra S. chose to consider:
Whether or not to continue to participate?

Question #1:

Coming from Fear, why would I not continue in the **Chi-To-Be! Masters Coaching Program?**

I find it hard to keep up with the assignments. I feel like I am not operating at my best here. I'm concerned that my lack of energy would bring the group down.

Question #2:

Coming from Love, why would I not continue in the
Chi-To-Be! Masters Coaching Program?
I have a lot on my plate right now. I could give myself a break by not continuing and direct my energy elsewhere.

Question #3: :

Coming from Fear, why would I continue in the
Chi-To-Be! Masters Coaching Program?
I would feel like a failure if I left. I would miss the coaching support. I would be afraid of failing without the guidance of my fellow Masters.

Question #4:

Coming from Love, why would I continue in the
Chi-To-Be! Masters Coaching Program?
Being part of the group has moved me forward in great ways. Each day I uncover more about myself. I don't have to be high energy to be here. I can just do my best and keep moving onward and upward. We all learn from each other no matter where we are on the journey. Coming from love I can be supported and support others. Coming from love I can schedule time for the assignments in smaller increments throughout the

week so I have enough energy and feel less
overwhelmed.

MY DECISION:

*To come from Love and continue growing
and changing and stay in the* **Chi-To-Be!**
Masters *Coaching Program. To be more
intentional in my planning and set aside
time each day for mastering my life.*

My Intentional Activity:

*Make contact with someone who wants to create a
Mastermind group with me to support each other in
developing our Plans, which will help me to be more
intentional in my planning.*

Corey S. was faced with this decision:
**Whether or not to move forward in recording a
mix tape immediately?**

Question #1:

*Coming from Fear, why would I not record the mix tape
immediately?*
I know that going to a recording studio is expensive,
and I want to be more financially stable before I pay
for a block of time.

Question #2:

*Coming from Love, why would I not record the mix tape
immediately?*

I love creating my music and I want to be in alignment and prepared mentally and financially because this project requires me to cross my T's and dot my I's, so to speak. I do love what I create so I will have to do all the legal stuff necessary so that no one else can take credit for it.

Question #3:

Coming from Fear, why would I record the mix tape immediately?
I have been putting recording off for long enough, and not being financially stable is a recurring issue, so I need to start recording to feel like I am moving forward in this vision, and not at a standstill.

Question #4:

Coming from Love, why would I record the mix tape immediately?
Coming from love, there is no need to rush. It will all come together when the time is right.

> **MY DECISION:**
> *I will record when the time is right.*
> *I will not rush the issue out of fear.*

My Intentional Activity:

I will continue to move forward in my vision in other ways, such as writing daily and networking with people. I also have to acknowledge the fact that I know how to record my own material with the proper resources. I will use the funds that would have gone into recording time to purchase a new laptop. In the long run, this will save me money.

Is Love Always The Answer?

I am often asked if the final answer will always be the one that comes from Love.

Actually, I've found that sometimes Fear feels much more powerful to us and that's perfectly alright. In this Process, there is no judgment, no right or wrong.

The Process works simply by listening to the answer that feels most powerful to you first as evidenced by **Chi-To-Be! Master Maria J.'s experience...**

> My son agreed to call a friend of his who works for an airline to get me a discounted ticket to spend Thanksgiving in Buffalo. He procrastinated so long that I cannot go. I decided to blame him entirely for this situation.
>
> **I came from Fear:** The fear said: "No one cares about me." Fear of being a discarded family member would cause me to behave in ways that would diminish my opportunity to be fair. Or: becoming a victim, which is an established pattern of behavior. I was also reluctant to travel because of financial issues. I felt that it would cause a financial difficulty to leave now, so I just let the details hang in the air. I never really prepared for the trip in my heart and mind. In fact, I did not prepare at all.
>
> **Coming from Love now:** I realize that I contributed to the procrastination because I was coming from Fear. I made a decision without making it. A very ineffective modus operandi! No decision is a decision.

The enormous emotional breakthrough I experienced was:

1) I have been hanging on to old patterns of behavior. One of which is to be hurt by other's behavior. What I realize now is blaming my son allowed me to excuse myself from making the decision not to visit my family. Although I feel devastated that I have not seen my grandson since his birth in February, I am in business for myself and I choose to be responsible regarding financial obligations.

2) The other face of the old pattern of behavior is attached to debilitating pain delivered through my family. I suddenly realized that I am part of causing my own pain. I am choosing to let go. By not taking things personally, I will have no reaction to other's behavior, I am free. I can now open my heart and forgive others because I realize that no one **intentionally** hurts me. Others are just doing their best. Opening my heart allows me to forgive myself because I am also doing my best.

My Intentional Activity:

#1: Using the 'The **Chi-To-Be! Solution Process**' decision-making process has helped me to see my part in everything that happens.. I am learning that letting details hang in the air creates a vortex that causes nothing to happen... It's a vortex of procrastination. I accept responsibility for my part in the failure of any venture.

#2: Employing 'The 4 Agreements' of don Miguel Ruiz. I realize that utilizing 'not taking things personally' and 'doing my best' opened the door to clearer thinking and revelation.

I am sure you can hear the power emanating from each of these decisions. What decision do you have in front of you right now?

I am inviting you to play with the Process. The next time someone asks you 'What Should I Do?,' please share this Process with them so that they, too, know that they always have a powerful tool for making their own decisions about their life!

• •

• • • • • • • • • • • RECAP • • • • • • • • • • •

1 The fastest way to achieve your *B-All* with ease is to make the most empowering decisions and choices as quickly as possible each and every time a decision or a choice arises.

2 The 4 questions of the **'Chi-To-Be! Solution Process'** are:

Question #1:
Coming from Fear, why would I not (fill-in-the-blank)?

Question #2:
Coming from Love, why would I not (fill-in-the-blank)?

Question #3:
Coming from Fear, why would I (fill-in-the-blank)?

Question #4:
Coming from Love, why would I (fill-in-the-blank)?

3 The **'Chi-To-Be! Solution Process'** is meant to be shared with anyone who asks 'What Should I Do?'. It is a powerful tool for making decisions in order to keep accomplishing **intentional activities** to fulfill **goals** on the way to achieving one's *B-All*.

chapter 11
Personal Accountability

> *"It is not only what we do, but*
> *also what we do not do, for*
> *which we are accountable."*
> Moliere

We began this book together at the end.   Now, we end the book at The Beginning…the beginning of a new relationship with yourself through the practice of **'Personal Accountability!'**

As I consider the word 'Accountability,' I feel strength and joy in the ability to be 'counted upon.'

Yet, when introducing the principle of 'Accountability' to my clients, they often share that they feel the principle of 'Accountability' is the same as 'Responsibility' and both are viewed through their relationships with others. In other words, both relate to what others expect of them.

They share with me that the feeling associated with be-ing 'accountable' and 'responsible' is heavy and un-inspiring – these words convey 'should' and 'duty' – and brings them back to their elementary school days of 'being responsible' to their teacher by doing their homework on time or to 'being responsible' to their father and mother for doing their chores by the time they said they would do them, or any other expectations that were put upon them which felt like weighty burdens. So, it's understandable that most of us can't wait to 'un-burden' ourselves of the heavy energy with which 'Accountability' and 'Responsibility' are associated when viewed from this perspective.

Yet, as a **Chi-To-Be! Energy Surge**, **Personal Accountability** has great energy and aliveness inherent within it when viewed instead from the question of "in what ways do I want to be counted upon by me?" And, this question, of course, connects me right back to Side #3 of the **Strategic Attraction Plan™** (Chapter 4) where I have already identified what I intend and desire to achieve, or attain, or be, or do towards the fulfillment of my *B-All*.

Over the past six years, one change that I have made (and which I now encourage the **Chi-To-Be! Masters™** to make) to my **Strategic Attraction Plans™**, is that I have changed the title of Side #3 to: 'I AM ....!' I have found the uplifting energy that arises from declaring myself to already be all the qualities, attributes, and achievements I listed on Side #3 provides me with strength to stay committed **(Accountable)** to fully be-ing and achieving what I have listed.

This new title of 'I AM...!' is the direct answer to the question: "in what ways do I want to be counted upon by me?

Even though I may not yet have achieved my *B-All* or all of my **goals**, I am able to declare and affirm – from my sense of **Personal Accountability** – that this is who I AM in my spirit and I AM committed to be accountable to me for creating **intentional activities** towards achieving these **goals**.

Here is my example of my Sample Side #3 from Chapter 4 now revised with the title of 'I AM!'"

(Bold items = items that are not yet achieved/accomplished)

Stacey's Side #3 Sample List

"I AM …!"

B-All:
– **A Doctor of Natural Medicine.**

Qualities:
– Trustworthy.
– Generous in spirit.
– Dependable.
– Believing that miracles occur in my life every day.
– Treating myself and others with respect.
– Enjoying collaborating and co-creating with others in ways that support us all to achieve our *B-All*.

Goals:
– **Attracting 4+ new essential oil distributor members to my team every week.**
– **Proficient at email, Facebook and Twitter.**
– **Always receiving an equal or greater exchange of energy for sharing my gifts with others.**
– **Easily and fully developing the programs and projects of Chi-To-Be!, LLC.**
– **Receiving and then depositing $xxx,000.00+ of revenues each month into my bank account for the next 50+ years from donations, sales and royalties of programs and projects I produce and/or facilitate, and these funds are always available to me for use as I desire.**

> ### Intentional Activities:
> – Replying to requests when it is perfect for me to do so.
> – Scheduling time daily to ask for and receive guidance from God and my concourse of angels to keep me always connected to the decisions that support my Highest Good.
> **– Creating and adding items to my Strategic Attraction Plan™ every day.**

When you compare this version with the one on Page 90, which one has a stronger sense of power and energy?

Personal Accountability Leads to Personal Responsibility

At this point, you may wish to review your own **Strategic Attraction Plan™** and begin to ask yourself: "What do I know I can already count on myself to give and/or provide to me in my life?" Then, add any new items to Side #3 of your Plan.

Next, ask yourself: "What do I wish I could count on myself to give and/or provide to me in my life?" Then, add those items to Side #3 of your Plan.

Some of these new additions which came from the answers to both questions might be personality *Qualities*. Some might be **goals**. Some might be **intentional activities** so take a moment to organize them...as well as highlight or **Bold** them since they are not yet fulfilled in the way that you intend them to be fulfilled.

Now consider whether you responded to my invitation above to ask yourself the two questions and if you added items to your Plan.

• • • • • • • • $\left[\begin{array}{c}\textit{Whether you did or did not --} \\ \textit{you responded.}\end{array}\right]$

Asking your self the questions was a direct response to my invitation.

Adding items to your Plan was a direct response to my invitation.

Choosing to not ask your self the questions and not adding items to my invitation was a direct response to my invitation.

Now, the question, 'what do I count on myself to give and/or provide to me in my life' comes into play.

Whichever one of these responses you gave, it is a direct indication of your own **Personal Accountability**...based upon what you want to be counted on to provide to yourself!

Personal Accountability gives each of us the ability to respond to others in ways that support ourselves in achieving our own *B-All.* When partnered with **Personal Accountability**, Responsibility becomes 'Response-ability' -- the ability to 'choose' to respond....or not respond... with ease and velocity!

Here's how I see **Personal Accountability** and Response-ability as a Process:

> **Step 1:** Identify what I want to be Accountable to be, do, or achieve towards my *B-All.*

Step 2: When Life brings an opportunity or a situation into my life, I first choose if I wish to respond or not respond...whichever will bring me closer to the fulfillment of my *B-All*.

Step 3: If I choose to respond, I do so in a way that moves me closer to the fulfillment of my *B-All*.

> ## IN ORDER TO CHOOSE HOW YOU WILL BE RESPONSE-ABLE, YOU MUST FIRST BE CONSCIOUS TO BE-ING PERSONALLY ACCOUNTABLE TO THE FULFILLMENT OF YOUR *B-All*!

For example, let's use a situation involving a mother of a small child.

Step 1: The mother has chosen to be **'Personally Accountable'** for keeping her child safe towards her *B-All* of raising a healthy, happy, enlightened human being to maturity.

Step 2: One night, she awakens suddenly and smells smoke. Upon further examination, she becomes aware that a fire has started in the kitchen. She is instantly consciously aware of her **'Personal Accountability,'** and she immediately chooses to 'respond' to the situation to ensure her child grows up to be a healthy, happy, enlightened human being.

Step 3: Her response: She rushes to her child's room and she quickly moves them both out of the house before calling the fire department.

Granted, this is an extreme situation of this Process, and yet it can be applied to every **activity** you choose to do or choose not to do throughout your day – from waking up, to brushing your teeth, from eating, to choosing which conversations you will have, to what you are charging for your services, etc.

To explain what I mean, I will give you an example from my own life.

As I have stated many times previously, my *B-All* is to achieve all the licenses and certifications required to be a Doctor of Natural Medicine. I am consciously **Personally Accountable** to me for achieving my *B-All*. One of the **goals** I have listed on Side #3 of my **Strategic Attraction Plan™** is: – I AM the care-giver of healthy and happy pets, who receive from me the perfect amount of care and attention to maintain their health and well being.

This means that I have chosen to be **Personally Accountable** for being the care-giver of healthy and happy pets, who receive from me the perfect amount of care and attention to maintain their health and wellbeing.

You may wonder how this **goal** supports me in achieving my *B-All* of being a Doctor of Natural Medicine. One very important way is that is essential that my home life be in balance along with the other aspects of my life…that I take care of my home life with ease and velocity. My husband and I chose to be the care-givers for three animals – 2 dogs and a cockatoo (who thinks he's a dog). This could be a huge distraction from achieving my *B-All* if I did not have it as a **goal** directly tied to achieving it.

By being **Personally Accountable** to ensuring my pets' well being through the perfect amount of care and attention, I am counting on myself to attract whatever is essential for providing that perfect amount of care and attention in harmony with my other **goals**. And, thank goodness, I did have this **goal** on my **Strategic Attraction Plan™** a couple of years ago.

One night, without warning, one of my dogs (Maggie) began having seizures. These events began on a Friday night with just one quick seizure that appeared as if she was having a bad dream since it happened while she was sleeping. I responded by waking her up, comforting her until she fell back to sleep and staying awake the rest of the night to ensure she was fine. While I was tired in the morning, she appeared to be just fine and I chose not to take her to the vet.

That evening, I made sure she was sleeping peacefully before I went to sleep. In the middle of the night, my husband and I were both awakened by the sound of her cage, in which she was sleeping, banging against the floor.

Maggie was experiencing another seizure and this one was much more violent than the one the night before. There was no doubt that I now had to respond by taking her to the animal clinic in the morning. After again staying awake until Maggie fell back to sleep and remaining awake to ensure she was alright until the morning (both response choices), Bill and I took her to see our vet who recommended to give her a prescription drug.

Earlier that morning, I had consulted my essential oils and other natural therapies books (another response choice) to identify what would be the best course of action if the vet determined that Maggie was having epileptic seizures. I had discovered in one of the books that this particular prescription drug was known to cause very serious side-effects. I shared this information with the vet, who confirmed my research. So, consciously aware of my **Personal Accountability**, I chose not to accept the prescription. The vet told me that there were other medications with fewer side-effects, but he was reluctant to start her on those because it would be more difficult to wean her off of them if she outgrew the seizures. He also said it was possible that Maggie might not ever have another seizure.

Based on that information, Bill and I chose to respond by taking Maggie home and watching to see if she had any other events before choosing to give her the medication.

Sure enough, Maggie had two more seizures that night. Bill and I decided to respond by researching veterinarians who used natural approaches and found one that could see her the next day.

The new vet explained to us that her response was to give Maggie another prescription medication, but in such a small dose that it would be easy to wean her off the drug when she outgrows the seizures. She confirmed, based on her research, that the seizures were likely to have been brought on by the combination of vaccinations that Maggie had received all at the same time a week prior to the episodes....vaccines that had been given by the first vet, whose response was to refute the possibility that this was the cause.

Since that time, we have changed the food we give Maggie to be grain-free (response choice), I anoint her with essential oils (response choice) and we are still giving her the medication twice daily (response choice) because she still will experience tremors when she is off the medication for any length of time. And, both of our dogs will no longer receive vaccinations because our veterinarian provides other ways to protect their immune systems (response choice).

I return now to being **Personally Accountable** for the **goal** of being the care-giver of healthy and happy pets, who receive from me the perfect amount of care and attention to maintain their health and wellbeing and how it relates to my *B-All*. Throughout the experience of discovering Maggie's seizures and how to appropriately care for her in response to my **Personal Accountability**, I was always conscious that learning how to use essential oils and other alternative approaches for a condition with which I had no previous experience would be a valuable **intentional activity** towards my **goal**.

This awareness transformed my fears which arose over Maggie's condition into another commitment to my self **(Personal Accountability)** to obtain and master more knowledge and skills in the use of essential oils and other natural approaches to wellness. I responded by creating a new **goal** of obtaining my certification as an Aromatherapy Coach and a Certified Raindrop Technique Practitioner (I completed the **intentional activities** associated with this **goal** and have obtained these certifications). With these certifications, as well as my License as a Spiritual Healer, I have moved three steps closer towards becoming a Doctor of Natural Medicine. Plus, I have attracted many opportunities for me to share the benefits of essential oils and other natural methods with more people than I was attracting before obtaining this knowledge and these credentials…clearly movement forward towards the fulfillment of my *B-All*.

Personal Accountability and the Success of All the Chi-To-Be! Energy Surges

Personal Accountability is at the core of every response – or 'non-response' – each of us makes throughout each and every day. How and when you choose – or choose 'not' – to practice and utilize each of the **Chi-To-Be! Energy Surges** will be determined by your own **Personal Accountability**. Any agreements that you have made to utilize the Energy Surges in this book are simply – and most importantly – agreements you have made with yourself. In other words, **Personal Accountability** is the tool that will make the other tools, tips and resources in this book produce success for you.

Personal Accountability is the answer to the question I am often asked most by my clients when they begin practicing the other Energy Surges.

This question they ask is: "Why did I not achieve my **goal** by when I intended even though I created my **Strategic Attraction Plan™** and I stayed positive?

• • • • • • • •
$$\left[\begin{array}{c} \textit{My answer is always:} \\ \textit{"Where were you not completely} \\ \textit{accountable to yourself?"} \end{array} \right]$$

I then begin to support them in identifying in what areas of their life they were not yet strong enough to count on doing what they said they would do. By strengthening our relationship to our self, we become stronger in attracting to us what we desire.

One of the ways to strengthen our relationship with our self is to use the **CHI GENERATOR CALCULATOR™** you will discover in Chapter 12. With this tool, you can monitor and measure on a daily basis how much energy you are generating to achieve your **goals** with velocity and ease by identifying how many of the **Chi-To-Be! Energy Surges** you are utilizing and how often towards achieving your *B-All*.

Personal Accountability Partnerships

When I am first learning how to count on myself in a new area of **Personal Accountability**, having the support of someone I trust who I know has my best interests at heart is essential. I always remember that I will likely 'do it poorly' at the beginning, and I create and schedule an **intentional activity** to ask these people to be my **Personal Accountability** Partners to support me in staying true to what I want to be able to count on me to be or accomplish. My **Personal Accountability** Partners assist me in utilizing the **Chi-To-Be! Energy Surges** to re-energize my energy when it begins to wane. They listen to ensure that I speak only positive encouragement to myself. They check-in with me to ensure I stay on track to accomplishing the **intentional activities** I schedule for me to accomplish towards my **goals**. This is how and why the **Chi-To-Be! Mastery Coaching Program™** came into existence…to support as many people as possible in attracting their own Personal Accountability Partnerships!

During a recent **Chi-To-Be! Masters** group coaching call, one of the Masters was late to the call for the second month in a row. After being late the first time, and because participating in the calls and receiving the value from the calls is an **intentional activity** towards her *B-All*, she responded by making a commitment to her self (**Personal Accountability**) and the group to be on time for all future group coaching calls. However, she did not write this as a **goal** on her **Strategic Attraction Plan™** and she did not consciously create **intentional activities** to support the **goal**.

When she was late to the call the second time, she responded first by acknowledging to me and her fellow Masters that she did not yet have the strength to be counted on to keep this commitment to her self. She let us know that she wanted the support of her 'Accountability Partners'. Next, because she made a commitment (**Personal Accountability**) to the Agreements of the **Chi-To-Be! Mastery Program,** one of which is to be on time for all group coaching calls, she was faced with a response choice – to choose to continue to be late, which would automatically cancel her Agreement to participate in the Program, or to create and schedule more **intentional activities** to strengthen her ability to count on her self to be on time for the calls.

She utilized '**The Chi-To-Be! Solution Process**' to make her decision. Her response choice was to create more **intentional activities** to strengthen her ability to count on herself to be on time for the calls. These **intentional activities** included upgrading her phone to ensure the alarm setting works every time, scheduling on her calendar to go to bed earlier the night before the monthly group coaching calls, and adding these **intentional activities** to Side #3 of her **Strategic Attraction Plan™** .

Here are more breakthroughs that have been achieved with velocity and ease with the support of Personal Accountability Partners as shared by a few the **Chi-To-Be! Masters** who offer their insights on practicing the questions asked earlier in this chapter regarding **Personal Accountability**...

 Maria J.

> *"Accountability...The key to my success. I believe that. I rarely make promises to others unless I am sure I can keep those promises. I am account-able at work and never (I can say 'never') miss an appointment with a client. When I am with a client I am accountable for the service I provide to them. My focus is 100% on their needs and on a beneficial outcome. My success in my business is somewhere between **Sprouting** and **BLOOMING** as a result. I now chose to be **Personally Accountable** to keeping my commitments to my clients to maintain a certain level of income to support myself. Last week I was only one client away from my* **goal** *of 15. From now on, I also count on myself to cook and shop*

for myself, to lose weight, to allow time in my schedule for the shopping, the cooking, and especially for adequate rest. I also count on me to remember: I always do my best!"

Sandra S.

*"A recent work experience was difficult for me because I was asked to take on projects for which I did not want to be counted upon to do. I was hired to update the organization's social media and technology format, which is exactly what I wanted to be counted upon to do. Unfortunately, I did not have an opportunity to demonstrate my skills because of the other duties I was expected to perform. I take **Personal Accountability** for responding willfully to these other tasks because I wanted to have some time to learn the workings of the office and develop my own time frame in accomplishing some of my duties. I acknowledge my responsibility that I was not as accurate on some things as I wanted to be. At the same time, from my **Personal Accountability**, I was responsible for arriving a half hour early each day, staying late, and making the kitchen area user-friendly so that we could have a good place to make coffee/tea and heat up food. In my short time in this position, I was **Personally Accountable** for upgrading the computer services, overseeing a major office move, coordinating a large pledge mailing and a Christmas production. I am currently becoming more aware of my **Personal Accountability** in setting **goals** and **intentional activities** for doing what I say I will do in a more timely fashion, for how I deal with difficult issues, and for being more fully engaged in life."*

D_{eZ} O.

"What I learned through this exercise is Accountability begins with me being response-able to myself first above all else! I had several opportunities with friends and my son to explore the differences in what accountability means to different people and the degree of its importance to them. There was no right or wrong view, just different. In one conversation, I was inspired to listen and feel how I might set myself up for the possibility of disappointment when I attempt to live up to another's expectations of me….a good reminder that Accountability begins and ends with me. When I know I am giving from my own intention to always provide the very best to friends/family/clients, and ultimately to myself, then I feel I that am "Be-ing" totally in the act of Personal Accountability."

T_{ara} R.

"I found from the feedback I received, I know I am delivering on what I wanted to be counted upon to provide/be/do ('Healthy Living,' mother, wife, friend, etc.), and that feels nice. I smiled when my daughter and a few others said, 'Well, I can't count on you for feeding me junk food.' So that statement became a way to restate what I do deliver on. Sometimes I catch myself feeling that I 'should' respond to others 'wishes' for me. For example, "I wish you knew the answer to EVERY question I have" or "I wish you could be here daily to help me get through the day" or "I wish you still lived here." Again, as a coach, and even with my family, I count on myself to always do my best to find an answer, but sometimes I just don't know the answer. I can only do my best. Recently, I asked a friend to be my exercise partner. Regular exercise fell to the wayside late last year when I was finishing projects, so that is a priority area for my Personal

Accountability. Unfortunately, I could not count on this particular person, so I am still creating intentional activities *to support me in be-ing* Personally Accountable *to myself in this area. Be-ing* Personally Accountable *to the agreements of the* Chi-To-Be! Program *has been the first time in a long time I have chosen to be Accountable to me and responding to stay on task in general. My biggest challenge is keeping my* goals *and* intentional activities *focused on my* B-All. *I do feel a sense of* Personal Accountability *in that I have responded by agreeing to complete assignments and the group support gives me an extra push to make it happen. Because I am still becoming more Accountable to me, sometimes solo self-commitments are still harder to keep than the ones in which I include and participate with others."*

• • • • • • • • • • **RECAP** • • • • • • • • • • •

"With accountability, we can rely upon ourselves. Others can also rely on us, because we are answerable for our actions. We are guided by our highest standards.

I take responsibility for my choices.
I have the humility to face my mistakes.
I am a lifelong learner.
I make amends.
I weigh both positive and negative outcomes.
I live up to my sense of justice.

Accountability is the willingness to stand in responsibility for every choice. It is acting with integrity, doing what we say we will do. When we make a mistake we do not seek to hide it or avoid it. We have the courage to face it willingly. We are open to the lessons it can bring, and ready to make amends. With accountability, people can rely on us, because we are answerable for our actions.

We appreciate both the good we have done and the good to be gleaned from the choices that do not turn out right. We are guided by our highest standards." – *Virtues Project International*[1]

[1] *Excerpted from Virtues Reflection Cards, by permission from Virtues Project International www.virtuesproject.com*

chapter 12
How Much Energy Are You Generating?

GENERATING ABUNDANT ENERGY TO ACHIEVE YOUR GOALS WITH VELOCITY AND EASE

Having now learned each one of the **11 Chi-To-Be! Energy Surges™** it is possible to monitor and measure how much energy you are generating to achieve your **goals**.

On a scale with '1' being equivalent to a complete lack of energy and '10' being equivalent to an abundance of energy to implement **intentional activities** towards the fulfillment of your **goals** towards achieving your *B-All*, what is the rating you would give to yourself and why?

Since each of us is our own energy generator, my encouragement to you is to set an **intentional activity** of utilizing the following **Chi Generator Calculator** at the start of your week – every week – to ensure that you have pumped up your power to its fullest. Then, as you Recapitulate and Cast (see Chapter 7) at the end of each day, use this Calculator to re-generate the energy that you expended during that day so that your energy remains abundant and vibrant…to ensure that your **goals** and *B-All* are achieved with the greatest velocity and ease!

CHI GENERATOR CALCULATOR

Once you have completed each item below, give yourself the number of amps associated with the item:

- **25 amps** = you have identified and/or remembered your *B-All* (Chapter 1)

- **25 amps** = you have identified and/or consciously spent time focusing on all the **goals** to be achieved on the way to your *B-All* (Chapter 1)

- **25 amps** = for each **goal** you have selected and set an intent to achieve this month.
  1 **goal** = 25 amps, 2 **goals** = 50 amps, etc (Chapter 1)

- **20 amps** = for every 2 **intentional activities** towards each of your **goals** to be implemented this week
  1 **goal**/2 **intentional activities** = 20 amps,
  two **goals**/ 4 **intentional activities** = 40 amps, etc.
  (Chapter 2)

- **10 amps** = you have identified the stage that your **goal(s)** is/are currently in right now (Chapter 3)

- **25 amps** = you have created a **Strategic Attraction Plan**™ to stay focused on attracting the people who will support you in achieving your **goals** with velocity and ease (Chapter 4)

■ **10 amps** = for each one of 'The Four Agreements®' you are intentionally practicing this week.
1 Agreement = 10 points, 2 Agreements = 20 points,
3 Agreements = 30 points, 4 Agreements = 40 points
(Chapter 5)

■ **10 amps** = for creating your own **'Loving 33 Ways System'**
(Chapter 6)

■ **10 amps** = for each time you go 'A.P.E.' this week.
1x = 10 amps, 2x = 20 amps, etc. (Chapter 6)

■ **10 amps** = for each tangible **intentional activity** you implement to express gratitude and appreciation for what you have already attracted this week. 1 **activity** = 10 amps, 2 activities = 20 amps, etc. (Chapter 6)

■ **10 amps** = for each time you implement a **Chi Generating Ritual** this week. 1x = 10 amps, 2x = 20 amps, etc. (Chapter 7)

■ **10 amps** = for each time you clear clutter this week.
1x = 10 amps, 2x = 20 amps, etc. (Chapter 8)

■ **5 amps** = for each **rest stop** you implement this week.
1x = 5 amps, 2x = 10 amps, etc. (Chapter 9)

■ **25 amps** = for each time you utilize the **'Chi-To-Be! Solution Process'** to determine the solution to a dilemma or decision you must make this week. 1x = 25 amps, 2x = 50 amps, etc. (Chapter 11)

*On a scale of 1 – 10:

Less than 25 amps = **1**
26 – 50 amps   = **2**
51 – 75 amps   = **3**
76 – 100 amps   = **4**
101 – 125 amps   = **5**
126 – 150 amps   = **6**
151 – 175 amps   = **7**
176 – 200 amps   = **8**
201 – 250 amps   = **9**
251+ amps = **10**

chapter 13
Being A Self-Generator of Abundant Energy

BECOMING A SELF-SUSTAINING GENERATOR OF ABUNDANT ENERGY

The **11 Chi-To-Be! Energy Surges** shared throughout this book are each provided to support you in raising and maintaining your energetic vibration so that you are fully empowered to implement your **intentional activities** towards your **goals** to achieve your *B-All* with velocity and ease.

I thank you for purchasing this book as one of your power tools. To show my appreciation, I have a free gift for you. Read to the end of this chapter for details about your free gift.

The book you are holding is just one component of an entire program designed to assist you in becoming a self generating powerhouse of abundant energy – one whose power is completely unaffected by the energy drains and black-outs of others. And, you know who in your life I am talking about!

The power tools of the **Chi-To-Be! System** are:

*"Chi-To-Be!'s Energy Surges to Achieve Your Goals with Velocity and Ease!":

A six-episode audio series of coaching sessions conducted with the **Chi-To-Be! Masters.** Each session features a discussion of the various 11 **Chi-To-Be! Energy Surges** featured in this book. Consider this a self-guided coaching session with me. As I facilitate each session, use my questions to amp up your personal power. Receive greater insights about each one of these powerful tools by listening to the discoveries and explorations shared by those who have been mastering these self-generating techniques.

How to order: Call Life Science Publishing at 1.800.336.6308 to discuss a program that meets your needs.

*"Chi-To-Be!'s Becoming a Self-Sustaining Generator of Energy – More Energy Surges to Achieve Your Goals with Velocity and Ease!":

Beyond the first 11 Chi-To-Be! Energy Surges, I discovered 12 more vibration-boosting methods, strategies and techniques. I and the Chi-To-Be! Masters™ will facilitate your exploration of each one of these power-producing tools during this audio series of 12 half-hour episodes.

How to order: Call Life Science Publishing at 1.800.336.6308 to discuss a program that meets your needs.

*Chi-To-Be!'s Mastery Coaching Program

If you are wondering how you can become a **Chi-To-Be! Master** and you know you are ready to be unstoppable in achieving your *B-All* with velocity and ease, I designed this Program for you. As a participant in the Mastery Coaching Program, you will receive personalized attention from your coach and group training support to identify and repair the energy drains and power leaks that are keeping you from being a fully self-sustaining generator of your own chi energy. The power tools of the **Chi-To-Be! Mastery Program** are this book, both audio series described above, a specially designed workbook created for the Mastery Program, as well as private or group coaching sessions.

How to order: Call Life Science Publishing at 1.800.336.6308 to discuss a program that meets your needs.

Free Gift: To say thank you for purchasing this book, my gift to you is one complimentary session of "**Chi-To-Be!'s Mastery Coaching Program.**" Yes, this session is absolutely free to you and there is no obligation to enroll in the Mastery Coaching Program. Use this session to boost the power you have generated from the **Energy Surges** you have discovered in reading this book. To schedule your complimentary session, please:

How to order: Call Life Science Publishing at 1.800.336.6308 to discuss a program that meets your needs.

I look forward to hearing from you as you achieve your **goals** and *B-All*. Please send an email to stacey@chi-to-be.com.

Appendix

MY STRATEGIC ATTRACTION PLAN™
FOR ATTRACTING
CHI-TO-BE! MASTERS

SIDE 1: The Qualities of my Perfect Chi-To-Be! Masters

- They have a *B-All* that they are fully intending to achieve with velocity and ease
- They are accountable to themselves to fulfill their *B-All* and respond appropriately from their Personal Accountability
- They register, pay, fully participate and are a perfect fit for the **Chi-To-Be Mastery Coaching Program** facilitated through Life Science Publishers
- They register through any of the **intentional activities** implemented to attract new **Chi-To-Be! Masters**
- They pro-actively implement their own **intentional activities** to be healthy and balanced in body, mind, emotions and spirit
- They enjoy and fully participate with their **Chi-To-Be! Mastery Coach**
- They receive and enjoy practicing the **Chi-To-Be! Energy Surges**
- They purchase and read '**Chi-To-Be! Achieving Your Ultimate *B-All***'
- They purchase and practice with both **Chi-To-Be!** audio

coaching programs
- They purchase **'Chi-To-Be! Achieving Your Ultimate B-All'** for 5+ of their friends
- They contact me to share and celebrate their movement towards their *B-All*
- Their energy is delightful for me to be around
- They are motivated by the energy of love
- They are kind in manner, speech and intention
- They are considerate of others' feelings
- They are responsible for themselves and practice healthy self-care
- They enjoy, acknowledge, and appreciate the support and information provided to them through the **Chi-To-Be! Mastery Coaching Program**
- They boost my energy and contribute to my wellness in wonderfully uplifting ways
- Their energy and **intentional activities** support me in achieving my *B-All* and my **goals**
- They set monthly **goals** towards the fulfillment of their *B-All* and they stay consciously connected to their **goals** throughout each month using the support of their **Chi-To-Be! Mastery coach** and the **Chi-To-Be! Energy Surges**
- They use the support of their **Chi-To-Be! Mastery coach** and the **Chi-To-Be! Energy Surges** to remain focused on each of their **goals** through all of its Stages of Growth until those **goals** are fulfilled and their *B-All* is achieved
- They are careful and conscious in their dealings with me and others
- They make it easy to be supported in achieving their *B-All* with ease and velocity by responding to coaching phone calls, emails, and text messages within 24 hours and taking immediate action on their **intentional activities**.
- They are proficient at email, Meetup, Facebook, LinkedIN, Twitter and other social media communication tools

- They participate and add their energy to our **Chi-To-Be!** groups and fan pages on Facebook and LinkedIn and tweet daily about the breakthroughs they are experiencing through the **Chi-To-Be! Mastery Program**
- They are trustworthy
- They are generous in spirit
- They have a prosperity and appreciation mindset
- They believe that miracles occur in their life every day
- They have a strong support system that they use to stay focused, centered, and in action towards their *B-All*
- They welcome and take advantage of opportunities the Universe provides to grow on a mental, emotional, physical and spiritual level.
- They treat themselves and others with respect
- Their word is their bond; they do what they say they will do when they say they will do it or they proactively request to change their agreement
- They treat their body like a magnificent temple to be cherished and pampered
- Each month, they each refer 1+ people who register, pay, fully participate and are a perfect fit for the **Chi-To-Be! Mastery Coaching Program**
- They open their own Young Living® essential oils Distributor account through http://www.youngliving.org/chitobe
- Their support generates for me $xxx,000.00+ each and every month in positive cash flow revenue into my bank account for the next 50+ years from donations, sales and royalties of programs and projects I produce and/or facilitate, and these funds are always available to me for use as I desire.

• •

SIDE 2: What Makes Me Tick

To make God smile every day

• •

SIDE 3: I AM....!

**Bold items = items that are not yet 100%
achieved/accomplished exactly as I intend**

MY *B-ALL*
- **I am a licensed Doctor of Natural Medicine**

Qualities
- Personally Accountable
- Trustworthy.
- Generous in spirit.
- Dependable.
- Believing that miracles occur in my life every day.
- Treating myself and others with respect.
- Enjoying collaborating and co-creating with others in ways that support us all to achieve our *B-Alls*
- A catalyst and I will stir up breakthroughs that may look like breakdowns in others' lives as I support them in achieving their *B-All* with velocity and ease
- A catalyst in my own life and will be experiencing my own breakthroughs that look like breakdowns as I achieve my *B-All* with velocity and ease
- Enjoying my prosperity and appreciation mindset
- Enjoying my strong support network I use to stay focused, centered, and in action towards my *B-All*
- Motivated by the energy of love
- **Kind in manner, speech and intention**
- **Considerate of others' feelings**
- **Practicing healthy self-care**
- **Intentionally healthy and balanced in body, mind, emotions and spirit**
- **Welcoming and taking advantage of opportunities the Universe provides to grow on a mental, emotional, physical and spiritual level.**

- Always aware, confident, and bring wellness, healing and harmony with me wherever I go and others benefit from these gifts

Goals
- A Licensed Spiritual Healer, a Certified Aromatherapy Coach, and a Certified Raindrop Technique™ practitioner
- Attracting 1000+ new Chi-To-Be! Masters from around the world to register, pay and fully participate and who are a perfect fit for the Chi-To-Be! Mastery Coaching Program every week
- Attracting 20+ new Young Living® essential oil distributors from around the world to my team every week through http://www.youngliving.org/chitobe
- Celebrating 'Chi-To-Be! Achieving Your Ultimate *B-All*' is #1 on the New York Times Best-Selling Books List and #1 on Amazon's Best-Selling Books List
- Proficient at email, Facebook, LinkedIn and Twitter and other social networking tools
- Always receiving an equal or greater exchange of energy for sharing my gifts with others.
- Easily and fully developing the programs and projects of Chi-To-Be!, LLC.
- Sharing with thousands of people around the world how to honor and care for their physical, emotional, mental, and energy bodies
- Treating my body like the magnificent spiritual temple it is and take perfect care of this temple so that each body is functioning at its optimal level of health
- Creating my websites with ease and they produce additional revenue streams for me
- Traveling with my husband when and how we desire
- Living in a home that I love and I feel is a perfect environment for achieving my *B-All*
- The care-giver of healthy and happy pets, who receive

from me the perfect amount of care and attention to maintain their health and wellbeing.

- Joyfully receiving the support of assistants and collaborators who perfectly, happily and with ease and grace make it possible for me to achieve my *B-All* with velocity in exchange for providing my services to them to support them to fulfill their *B-All*
- Actively supporting all of my perfect Young Living® distributor team members in the most productive and efficient ways for achieving their *B-All*
- Joyfully receiving and then depositing $xxx,000.00+ each and every month in positive cash flow revenues into my bank account for the next 50+ years from donations, sales and royalties of programs and projects I produce and/or facilitate, and these funds are always available to me for use as I desire.

Intentional Activities

- 'Scheduling for Success' what I do daily according to what supports me in achieving my *B-All* as quickly as possible
- Practicing my Chi-Generating Rituals morning and night
- Requesting and receiving guidance from God and my concourse of angels daily to keep my always connected to the decisions that support my Highest Good.
- Reading and using the principles shared in '**Chi-To-Be! Achieving Your Ultimate *B-All*'** every day
- Scheduling and facilitating coaching calls daily and monthly
- Replying to correspondence when it is perfect for me to do so
- Posting and adding my 'chi lifts' to the **Chi-To-Be!** groups on Facebook and LinkedIn 3+/week
- Requesting and receiving coaching and 'chi lifts' to clear any upsets and breakdowns I experience within the same day
- Spending 5 minutes/day reviewing my Strategic Attraction Plan™

- Writing the **Chi-To-Be Intentional Activity** Experience **Tip** to post on my website every Sunday
- Setting monthly **goals** towards the fulfillment of my *B-All* and staying consciously connected to my **goals** throughout each month using the support of my fellow **Chi-To-Be! Masters** and the **Chi-To-Be! Energy Surges**
- Focusing on and practicing **1+ Chi-To-Be! Energy Surge each week** to remain focused on each of my **goals** through all of its Stages of Growth until those **goals** are fulfilled and my *B-All* is achieved
- Participating in a family meeting 1+/week to co-create with my husband a stable and happy home life
- Eating 3 meals each day and taking my nutritional supplements with each meal
- Hosting my weekly internet radio show to share information about how to use essential oils
- Facilitating 1+ NIA class each week
- Spending ½ hour every day playing catch with Maggie and Tess
  Walking 3+/week with Bill
- Maintaining my Young Living® distributor account in good standing each and every month with orders of $100+ each month
- Meeting with my nutritionist 2x/month
- Scheduling **rest stops** every 2 hours every day between 8:00 a.m. and 10:00 p.m.
- Scheduling chatting/spending time with 1+ friends every day
- **Turning off the computer at 10:00 p.m. every night to take a rest stop before going to sleep**
- **Keeping my Chi flowing by clearing clutter every day**
- **Presenting/facilitating 1+ workshop, seminar, gathering each week to support others in learning how to enhance and maintain their wellness using the Chi-To-Be! Energy Surges and/or essential oils**

- Meeting 1+ times/week with my assistants and collaborators who perfectly, happily and with ease and grace make it possible for me to achieve my *B-All* with velocity in exchange for providing my services to them to support them to fulfill their *B-All*

••

SIDE 4: What I Am In The Process of Improving to be More Attractive

Everything in **bold** on Side #3

Chi-to-Be!™ Masters

Olivia P. Biera, Chief, OPB Consulting

My *B-All*:
To ensure my daughter's wellbeing, prosperity, health and strong spiritual connection, while refining my own through core connection to Highest Truth and Deepest Body Consciousness so that we are able to do the work to hold the Earth in balance.

The Most Important Thing In The World To Me Is:
The journey to reach Deepest Body Consciousness and Highest Truth for evolution and resonance through relating to family and service.

*Participating in the **Chi–To-Be! Mastery Program** has been one of the best decisions I have made for myself and my business. I AM Olivia Perez Biera, founder of OPB Consulting, offering assistance in various aspects of Alternative Healing. As a Facilitator, Practitioner, Instructor, and Consultant, I have found continued inspiration and direction through many modalities. I made the choice to participate in this Program because I had been traveling a lot and felt the need to ground myself and get back on track with some of the business projects that I had put on hold.*

Exceeding my expectation, the group participation and the one-on-one coaching have played an equally important role in penetrating into the core of refining my own mastery. Specifically, the Program has been helping me to apply what I know in the heart of my hearts, by living each moment as an **intentional activity** *towards my immediate and ultimate* **goals**. *The skills and tools shared in this Program helped me to ground, center and focus, with the added bonus of floating into an energy that creates 'velocity and ease' in the fulfillment of my projects.*

Another magnificent result has been the true mental organization of living out all of my **goals** *in integrity with my artistry, which has in turn created such a deep sense of peace for me. I am truly 'great full' for pushing myself to make the commitment to join, and especially for Stacey Hall's commitment to my success.*

Whatever the circumstance or results to be achieved, by committing to and fulfilling this program, the results will be a positive wave for the future. In my case, there are results in my personal and professional life that excelled my own imagination and have sparked new visions and opened pathways for their fulfillment. How exciting it is to be a part of this evolution and escort others as well. Thank you!

Contact me at: 213-272-7451
http://www.opbconsulting.com/

••

Loralee Humpherys, LMT

My *B-All*:
To create an online Educational and Wellness Center that Teaches, Touches and Trains individuals, inspiring a change of consciousness in them that leads to lifestyle behaviors and habits that encourage and support Health and Longevity.

The Most Important Thing In The World To Me Is:
Sovereignty of Being (freedom of time and movement) – taking full responsibility for that which I co-create in my life.

As I become more conscious and accountable to myself, more of my time and energy is focused on those activities that are in alignment with what I feel is my life's purpose and work.

*One outcome I have achieved from participating in the **Chi-To-Be! Mastery Program** is the decision to return to school and become a Nutritional Consultant. As I move deeper into this current phase of my learning, I recognize that the next steps for me include walking fully on my own and embracing my leadership capacities. One of the ways in which this manifested in my life was the recognition of when it was time for me to graduate from the Program.*

*I continue to implement the principles and tools learned though this Program. I hold energy for all those utilizing this Program to achieve their own **B-All** and to know when it is your time to step fully into your own strength of accomplishment. I wish for you what I achieved – the fulfillment of my deepest heart's desires with abundance, grace and ease.*

Contact me at: 702-461-9533,
Loralee@energiesinmotion.com

Maria Jackson, LMT, BA, MA

My *B-All*:
To build a refuge for those who have found
Western medicine has failed them.

**The Most Important Thing In The
World To Me Is:**
To be free to be myself.

*I chose to participate in the **Chi-To-Be! Mastery Program** because I
was aware that the next leg of my journey would require support
and partnerships.*

*It is easier for me to be reclusive; therefore, seeking out
partnerships/relationships is not easy. Oh, I have no trouble making
friends and helping others; however, in the past, I have hidden
behind a facade of: "Oh, don't worry about me. I am capable of
handling anything that comes my way." Which translates into "Do
Not Enter." "No Trespassing."*

*I have benefited most from the personal coaching and the group
coaching calls. I chose to accept and practice the principles that Stacey
shared through the Program to open my heart. Because of this
opening I now believe that my dreams will be realized effortlessly
and with velocity.*

*I also believe that one can never learn anything alone. I see my
reflection in the mirror of the others with whom I interact. I
appreciate all my fellow **Chi-To-Be! Masters** – my 'partners in
success' – very much. With their assistance, my website –the first
important* **goal** *toward my B-All – is now in development.*

*My greatest breakthrough came through a deeper understanding of
where I am in relation to the success of others. I believed that I was*

"less than" those who had achieved success in their chosen area. I never looked at my own successes. I believed that I was out of the league of the successful. I now realize that everyone's success is in various stages of development; based upon the number of successful people I have attracted to me, I know my success will exceed my wildest dreams.

Contact me at: 702-769-8343, mj89119@aol.com

••

Lauren Kling

My *B-All*:
To change the world and people's lives in a positive and influential way and thus be financially successful and extremely happy.

The Most Important Thing In The World To Me Is:
To be happy and be the best person I can possibly be.

*When Stacey initially told me about the **Chi-To-Be! Mastery Program**, I was extremely excited! I graduated from UC Berkeley about two years ago and became a professional poker player. As much as I love my career, I intend to do more than just focus on poker. The aspect I enjoy most about participating in the Program has been my constant, rapid growth as a person. I have learned so much and my awareness, consciousness, and vibration have all risen as a result of participating. Each week, when I practice the tips and listen to the recordings, I continue to grow and improve my quality of life.*

*One of the most valuable benefits about the program was realizing the most important thing in the world to me and identifying my **B-All**. I always had an idea of what I wanted to do and this Program has assisted me in actually sitting down, thinking about it, and mapping out* **goals** *to achieve my **B-All**.*

*Since participating in this program I have achieved a plethora of results and seen many signs of land toward my **B-All**. For example, I learned how to be accountable to myself and not let my schedule dictate my life. I also learned that in order to achieve my **B-All**, I can set monthly* **goals** *and constantly update them in order to reach it faster. I learned to appreciate and be grateful for my life, the* *people, and the many amazing things in it. I learned to only associate with individuals who are positive influences. I learned how to change my language and thinking in a way that focuses on the positives, thus focusing all of my energy only on things that are beneficial to me. I learned how to create a **Strategic Attraction Plan**™* that has helped me attract a new backer, helped me realize what I truly want in all of my relationships, and has helped me attract the qualities I am desiring in many aspects of my life and career.*

This program has truly changed my life by assisting me to stay on the path to the achievement of my **goals** *and my B-All. I am so happy and honored I have had the opportunity to participate in it with all of the other Masters, who also have high* **goals** *and positive attitudes!*

Contact me at: laurkling@gmail.com,
http://www.twitter.com/laurenkling

Christina Lindley

My *B-All*:
To win a major live poker tournament with a $1 million+ cash award for first place. To use the winnings that I make to help people on a grand scale and change the lives of my family and friends.

The Most Important Thing In The World To Me Is:
To be successful.

*I chose to participate in the **Chi-To-Be! Mastery Program** because I intend my 'quality of life' to be as amazing as possible every day, which means I intend to become the best person I can be, constantly achieving a higher level of understanding about who I am and how to live my life to my fullest potential.*

*What I enjoy the most about the program is how I have used it to understand exactly who I was being in the past, and who I am now as a result of being my **B-All** and being consciously aware of my actions and intentions every day.*

Most valuable to me was reaching my **goals** *and achieving what I set out to do. I intended to become one of the best poker players in the world. I am now experiencing progress every day on my way towards that* **goal***:*

– I intended to attract a financial backer. I have.
– I intended to win a live tournament with a cash prize of over a million dollars. I expect to accomplish this **goal** *within the next year based on the results I have achieved since participating in this Program.*
– I also intend to use the wealth and notoriety I achieve to help my family and friends, and to improve the poker industry for

the better. I have already been able to make a difference in how I provide support to my family and friends. Making a difference in the Poker industry is next on my list of **goals.**

Contact me at: christinalindley@yahoo.com or christinalindley.net https://twitter.com/#!/lindleyloo

....

Valerie Melotti
Artistic Director - Dreamspell Studios

My *B-All*:
To support people so they can make educated choices about their health and their treatments.

The Most Important Thing In The World To Me Is:
Experiencing health through peaceful, loving feelings!

*I chose to join the **Chi-To-Be! Mastery Program** because I saw it as an opportunity to learn. This Program brings me great pleasure as it challenges and inspires me. I truly value the support I receive from my fellow Masters as we grow and learn together. Each day I celebrate the joy I experience on this journey.*

Since I joined this program, I am accomplishing my **goals** *with ease and velocity.*

Some I consider magnificent manifestations, like opening a recording/art studio. Others, minor miracles, such as becoming pregnant with my third child at exactly the time I desired. I have also achieved greater clarity and confidence in pursuing and fulfilling my dreams.

I believe that with appreciation, joy grows. I truly appreciate this powerful Program and I am honored to be a part of it.

Contact me at: http://www.dreamspellstudios.com

DeZ O'Connor, Certified Reiki Master & Teacher

My *B-All*:
My "Serenity Tea House"

The Most Important Thing In The World To Me Is:
Learning, sharing and teaching the power of Love for creating amazing successful manifestations in ALL aspects of life.

I am known as DeZ – 'The Rose Quartz Healing Mentor.' I teach how to manifest your dreams into reality by filling them with the power of LOVE in the same way you feel LOVE for those you hold dear in your heart. Watch the amazing blessings that will begin to occur.

*I believe the **Chi-To-Be! Mastery Program** chose me to participate through the Law of Attraction, even more than I chose to be in the Program. It was pretty much a 'slam dunk' deal you could say. Shortly after meeting Stacey, she shared with me the incredible book "Attracting Perfect Customers". I literally read the entire book in one day and began immediately creating several **"Strategic Attraction Plans**^{TM}**"*** with incredibly fast results.*

*To participate in this Program with Stacey was the natural next step for going beyond the Plans to learn how to apply the **Chi-To-Be!™ Energy Surges** to all areas of my life. What I 'in-joy' the most – as well as value the most – are our monthly group calls. The energy that is generated from supporting one another and just being together is exhilarating.*

*What I have already achieved towards my **B-All**: is continuous fine-tuning of my intentions, which always leads to attracting* *amazing opportunities that move me closer and closer to fulfilling my Serenity Tea House. Thank you, Stacey, and thanks to each of my fellow **Chi-To-Be! Masters** for continuing to inspire me to "BE ALL" that 'I AM'.*

Contact me at: Serenity Living Inspirations, www.serenitylivinginspirations.com; serenitylivinginspirations@gmail.com

....

* Attracting Perfect Customers, The Power of Strategic Synchronicity by Stacey Hall and Jan Brogniez, copyright © by Stacey Hall and Jan Brogniez, Published by Berrett-Koehler Publishers, Inc.

Tara Rayburn,
'The Healthy Habit Coach'

My *B-All*:
To create a "tidal wave of REAL Health" using all of the senses in order to inspire others to become "Healthy Ripples" in our world. I will achieve this while being a "present" and grounded wife and mother.

The Most Important Thing In The World To Me Is:
My relationship with God.

*I am a mother of two, wife of one, a 'Healthy Habit Coach', Speaker, Author, Weston A. Price Chapter Leader, Young Living® Essential Oil distributor and avid blogger. I organize Healthy Living experiences, and I aim to keep myself a clean conduit for God to do His work. I attracted the **Chi-To-Be! Mastery Program** into my life in the most perfect way and most perfect time. It has truly been an answer to prayers in the most pleasantly unexpected ways. The tips and 'Surges' cause me to stretch my thinking and "Being" beyond what I had previously thought possible.*

As 'The Healthy Habit Coach', I aspire to find and share wonderful tools for my clients. 'Chi-To-Be!' will certainly be one of the top books and programs I will recommend. It has helped me in profound ways both personally and professionally. I am a better coach for having been through such an amazing coaching experience.

What I love most about this Program is that it has a "living" and encompassing nature. This experience inspires growth in ALL aspects of my life. It is like watching a great movie with a wonderful twist or pay-off, only I am IN it...and it is Real.

*It is an absolute joy to see my dreams presenting themselves daily as I focus on my **B-All**, clarify WHO I AM, and create the* **goals** *and means to get there gracefully. I am enjoying a new way of life with my husband, children, friends and community.*

The blocks I had regarding financial prosperity and the magnitude at which I can make a difference in this world continue to be transformed. It is great to have big **goals**, *but even greater to be empowered with the tools to get there.*

Namaste, my fellow and future 'Chi-To-Be! Masters'!

Contact Me at: www.NourishingYourFamily.com,
Tara@NourishingYourFamily.com,
www.theHealthyHabitCoach.com

• •

Sandra Lee Schubert, MSC

My *B-All*:
To be known for my great work that inspires and motivates people to create their own great work and live an inspired life.

The Most Important Thing In The World To Me Is:
Knowing each day is full of possibility.

As a creative facilitator, radio host and producer I am able to combine my love of new media with a passion for showing people how they can get their word out through a variety of mediums. As a writer, interfaith and healing minister I provide a variety of unique skills to coach people to be heard online, on air and in person.

At the time I began my participation in the Chi-To-Be! Mastery Program, I was in a state of panic over my financial and living situation. I was feeling frustrated that the things I love to do were not the things bringing me cash at that moment. Through this Program, I have come to understand how I operated out of fear my entire life.

In the past it was hard to think of loving my customers when I didn't treat myself well. I abdicated responsibility for my part in the world when I felt insecure or less "the expert". One of the many benefits I have received from this program is that I first and foremost now love myself better.

I gained clarity about how to work my strategic plan for attracting perfect customers. I used to feel "bad" that I had to improve myself in some areas instead of acknowledging that I am learning new things all the time to grow and thrive as a person.

I am now a 'thriver,' rather than a survivor. I see myself asking better questions in a situation, planning my day around my strategic plan – rather then wishful thinking.

A good program will blow your mind. It will ask that you take what you have done and transform it in a big way. I recommend the **Chi-To-Be! Mastery Program** *because it does all this by supporting me to create the people, places and things that support the life I want to live.*

Contact me at: sandraleeschubert@gmail.com Visit my website: http://www.wildwomannetwork.com

....

Corey Stallings

My *B-All*:
To create my own entertainment company.

The Most Important Thing In The World To Me Is:
To learn so I can live joyous, free, creative, healthy, and abundant!.

From my perception living is learning. To learn is to grow. There is always room for growth. To share with others so that they can do the same is a wonderful gift to give!

*At the time I chose to be in the **Chi-To-Be! Mastery Program**, I had recently come to a crossroad in my life's journey. I decided to take the path toward my dream of becoming a recording artist and owning my own entertainment company, which will represent the passion and integrity of the artist and the art created. What I enjoy the most about my participation in the Program is the opportunity to share this experience with like-minded individuals, all with different* **goals***, yet all applying the tools practiced in this Program to achieve their own* **goals** *with ease.*

I am all for working smarter and not harder so learning and using the 'Energy Surges' provided was very valuable for me. As a result of my involvement in the Program, I have attracted many individuals with experience in the entertainment/music industry, who are in alignment with what I desire my company to represent and are willing to support me in any way. I am bringing the artistry back to the industry.

Contact me at: cls4505@yahoo.com, Alcoreybizz@gmail.com, and on Facebook™ at Corey Stallings

Michael Thrower, LSH/CRP/CAC

My *B-All*:
To reach financial freedom, study with the best minds in the world and bring this wisdom back to others.

The Most Important Thing In The World To Me Is:
To reach the highest level of consciousness where I am one with God and a channel for His Divine creativity.

I am a Licensed Spiritual Healer with certifications in the Raindrop Technique, Color Light Therapy, and a certified Aromatherapy Coach. My passions are empowering people's lives by helping them discover their dreams and then putting them in it, working with healing energy, music, meditation and life.

I firmly believe that nothing happens by accident. Stacey and I met at a Raindrop Technique intensive workshop and then continued to synchronistically meet at various workshops. During these experiences, I recognized her amazing talents and insights.

*My reasons for participating in the Program were to become clear about what I wanted to accomplish and to get assistance in getting there. Since joining the **Chi-To-Be! Mastery Program**, Stacey has helped me recognize and develop the skill set I need to take my life to where I want it to be. The tips and 'Energy Surges' gave me solid steps on which to build the foundation of growth to the fulfillment of my **B-All**.*

Now I am making progress towards reaching the Gold-level of Young Living® distributorship on my way to the ultimate level of

Crown Diamond. My own business, 'MindsEyeHome', is thriving.

I've not only found my dream, I am in it! What a blessing!

Contact me at:
http://mindseyehome.younglivingworld.com,
http://mindseyehome.com

....

About the Author
Stacey Hall

Stacey Hall is the author of *"Chi-To-Be! Achieving Your Ultimate B-All"* and the creator of the **Chi-To-Be!™ Mastery Program**.

She is also the co-author of the global best-seller *'Attracting Perfect Customers...The Power of Strategic Synchronicity,'* which has been translated into numerous languages since its publication in 2001 by Berrett-Koehler Publishers.

She is credited by industry experts as the creator and the catalyst for the **Strategic Attraction Planning Process™**.* Since she first began sharing this paradigm-shifting methodology in 1996, thousands of small business owners, corporate executives, entrepreneurs, as well as sales and training teams, have been transformed into powerful magnets that attract the most profitable customers and clients to their doors and web sites.

Stacey is a Licensed Spiritual Healer, a Certified Healing Coach, a Certified Aromatherapy Coach, a CARE-Certified Raindrop Technique Practitioner, and a Licensed and Certified NIA Technique Instructor. She is also the host of the weekly internet radio show 'AromaWellness in the Palm of Your Hand!'

She is the Owner and CEO of Chi-To-Be!, LLC, facilitating programs for individual and organizational productivity & wellness. Stacey is also a Distributor for Young Living® Essential Oils, and she is the Marketing Director for 'Bill Hall's One Stop for Las Vegas Homes Team of Realty One'.

In her own words:

My mission is to use my gifts, tools and resources to support those who intend to reach their **goals** with velocity and ease.

My *B-All* is to be a Doctor of Natural Medicine teaching thousands of people around the world how to honor and care for their physical, emotional, mental, and energy bodies before I leave this earth.

The Most Important Thing In The World To Me is be contributing positively and harmoniously towards the betterment of the World.

One of my top 3 **goals** I have set to achieve towards my *B-All* is the world-wide implementation of my **Chi-To-Be!™** coaching program designed to help develop the confidence and skills, as well as generate and maintain the inner and outer energy, necessary for the success of every person who has a *B-All* they feel they must achieve!

Please visit the Chi-To-Be! website:
http://www.chi-to-be.com

Another one of my current **goals** is to attain the Crown Diamond Level of Achievement with Young Living® by sharing the benefits and use of therapeutic-grade essential oils so everyone can give themselves the gift of wellness ... one drop at a time!

Listen to my weekly internet radio show 'AromaWellness in the Palm of Your Hand' at http://www.talkshoe.com/tc/31423 For more information about Young Living® therapeutic-grade essential oils, please visit my website at http://www.youngliving.org/chitobe

And, for more information about The NIA Technique, please visit http://www.NiaNow.com

Contact me at: stacey@chi-to-be.com
Twitter: http://twitter.com/#!/ChiToBe_Oils
Facebook: StaceyHall1

*As stated in "Attracting Perfect Customers, The Power of Strategic Synchronicity by Stacey Hall and Jan Brogniez, copyright © by Stacey Hall and Jan Brogniez, Published by Berrett-Koehler Publishers, Inc.

Index

Stacey Hall and Jan Brogniez

ATTRACTING PERFECT CUSTOMERS
The Power of Strategic Synchronicity

Most businesses spend far too much of their time and energy struggling to get new customers or hang on to existing ones—even customers who are ultimately more trouble than they're worth. *Attracting Perfect Customers* invites readers to move beyond the notions that "business is war" and winning market share means "beating" the other guy. Stacey Hall and Jan Brogniez outline a simple strategic process for making businesses so highly attractive that perfect customers and clients are naturally drawn right to them.

The authors lead you step by step through the entire strategic attraction process, revealing the six success standards of strategic synchronicity and sharing simple, fun, and easy-to-follow exercises that can be applied to any organization. You'll discover a place where there is an abundance of perfect customers and clients with whom you can build strong, satisfying, profitable, and lasting relationships.

> *"By connecting with the power of Strategic Synchronicity, your work will give you a much higher rate of return in satisfaction, productivity, and profitability."*

— Jack Canfield, coauthor of the #1 New York Times bestselling
  Chicken Soup for the Soul® series

> *"This is an incredibly insightful book with amazingly practical applications."*

— Brian Tracy, author of *Eat That Frog!*

Berrett–Koehler Publishers, Inc.
San Francisco
www.bkconnection.com

$22.95 • paperback • 224 pages
ISBN 978-1-57675-124-4
Also available as an e-book